This book is a

Gift

From

....

To

....

Date

....

May God bless you through this book

PRAYERS FOR FINANCIAL BREAKTHROUGH

PRAYER M. MADUEKE

PRAYERS FOR FINANCIAL BREAKTHROUGH

PRAYER M. MADUEKE

PRAYER PUBLICATIONS
1 Babatunde close, Off Olaitan Street,
Surulere, Lagos, Nigeria
+234 803 353 0599

PRAYERS FOR FINANCIAL BREAKTHROUGH
Copyright © 2013

PRAYER M. MADUEKE

ISBN:9781492917434

Prayer Publications

All rights reserved. No part of this work may be reproduced or transmitted in any form or by any means without written permission from the publisher

Unless otherwise indicated, all Scripture quotations are taken from the King James Version of the Bible, and used by permission. All emphasis within quotations is the author's additions.

First Edition, 2013

For further information of permission

1 Babatunde close, off Olaitan Street, Surulere, Lagos, Nigeria
+234 803 353 0599
Email: pastor@prayermadueke.com,
Website: www.prayermadueke.com

Table of Contents

1. Owners of evil load — 1
2. Warfare prayers section — 39

COMPREHENSIVE PRAYER LIST

- *Prayer for financial assistance* — 41
- *Prayer for financial breakthrough* — 45
- *Prayer for financial miracles* — 49
- *Prayer for divine breakthrough* — 53
- *Prayer for divine opportunities* — 56
- *Prayer for divine connections* — 60
- *Prayer for business breakthrough* — 66
- *Prayer for divine promotion* — 70
- *Prayer for prosperity* — 74
- *Prayer for protection from enemies* — 77
- *Prayer for protection from evil* — 81
- *Prayer deliverance from poverty* — 85
- *Prayer to overcome enemies in the place of work* — 89
- *Prayer to pay bills* — 93
- *Prayer to prosper in business* — 97
- *Prayer for divine connections* — 101
- *Prayer to prosper in foreign land* — 109
- *Prayer to recover lost businesses* — 116
- *Prayer to recover a lost job* — 120
- *Prayer to recover all your loss* — 124

- *Prayer to revive collapsed or collapsing business*   128
- *Prayer to revoke evil decrees*   133
- *Prayer to rise from defeat*   137
- *Prayer to search and find a job*   141
- *Prayer to stop determined enemies*   145
- *Prayer to succeed where others are failing*   149
- *Prayer to survive famine and economic meltdown*   153

DEDICATION

This book is dedicated to individuals and families, who are sincerely trusting God for financial breakthrough and management according to His Word.

"Then they cried unto the LORD in their trouble, and he saveth them out of their distresses. He sent his word, and healed them, and delivered them from their destructions" (Psalms 107:19-20).

Chapter 1

OWNERS OF EVIL LOAD

CHAPTER OVERVIEW
- *What is an evil load?*
- *Instances of evil load*
- *How to return evil loads to their owners*
- *Destined to overcome*
- *Spiritual warfare*
- *Provision, promise and victory*
- *Divine provision*
- *God promise, power and victory*
- *General prayers*

> "*⁷So went Satan forth from the presence of the LORD, and smote Job with sore boils from the sole of his foot unto his crown*" ([Job 2:7](Job 2:7)).

This passage, and several other passages, of the Scriptures have continued to confound many Christians, including bible scholars. How could Satan appear in the presence of the LORD, and even gained an audience from God? How could God have allowed that? Well, simply, only God knows. But one truth that played out in the above scripture is that Satan and all his demons are the chief sources of all sicknesses, afflictions and attacks on earth. They intend no good for any man. Although other causes of disasters can be argued, but Satan is at the helm of all evil and wickedness. Sin is his most successful weapon.

> "*⁴⁴Ye are of your father the devil, and the lusts of your father ye will do. He was a murderer from the beginning, and abode not in the truth, because there is no truth in him. When he speaketh a lie, he speaketh of his own: for he is a liar, and the father of it*" (John 8:44).

> "*¹⁴Afterward Jesus findeth him in the temple, and said unto him, Behold, thou art made whole: sin no more, lest a worse thing come unto thee*" (John 5:14).

God's plan and will for any man has never been of evil, but good. That's how we know that the frustration, confusion and depression most people go through are not from God, but from Satan, including all spiritual and physical problems. Since God expelled him from heaven, he hasn't relented but consistently attacked God's universe and God's people. He is the originator of all evil works, having recruited millions of humans into his army of evildoers. The Scriptures also called him the accuser of the brethren, adversary, ruler of darkness, sinner and murderer of good things and people on earth.

> "¹⁰And I heard a loud voice saying in heaven, Now is come salvation, and strength, and the kingdom of our God, and the power of his Christ: for the accuser of our brethren is cast down, which accused them before our God day and night" (Revelation 12:10).

> "⁸Be sober, be vigilant; because your adversary the devil, as a roaring lion, walked about, seeking whom he may devour" (1 Peter 5:8).

> "¹²For we wrestle not against flesh and blood, but against principalities, against powers, against the rulers of the darkness of this world, against spiritual wickedness in high places" (Ephesians 6:12).

> "⁸The wind bloweth where it listeth, and thou hearest the sound thereof, but canst not tell whence it cometh, and whither it goeth: so is every one that is born of the Spirit" (John 3:8).

Lucifer, as his name also was, is the father of all lies and evil worker. He can enter into any person's life through sin, idolatry, evil inheritance, consultation with familiar spirits, occultism, palm reading, hypnotism, witchcraft, etc. Equally, failure to resist him can prove to be detrimental.

> "¹⁴But the Spirit of the LORD departed from Saul, and an evil spirit from the LORD troubled him. ¹⁵And Saul's servants said unto him, Behold now, an evil spirit from God troubled thee" (1 Samuel 16:14-15).

> "²⁷Neither give place to the devil" (Ephesians 4:27).

> "⁷Submit yourselves therefore to God. Resist the devil, and he will flee from you" (James 4:7).

Whenever you cooperate with evil spirits or open your heart to occult practices, Satan quickly takes advantage of such opportunity to plant evil seeds in your life. And when you keep properties like charms, amulets, occult books, etc., in your house, Satan stays in your house to guard such materials.

"*²⁵And it came to pass the same night, that the LORD said unto him, Take thy father's young bullock, even the second bullock of seven years old, and throw down the altar of Baal that thy father hath, and cut down the grove that is by it: ²⁶And build an altar unto the LORD thy God upon the top of this rock, in the ordered place, and take the second bullock, and offer a burnt sacrifice with the wood of the grove which thou shalt cut down"* (Judges 6:25-26).

"*⁸Beware lest any man spoil you through philosophy and vain deceit, after the tradition of men, after the rudiments of the world, and not after Christ"* (Colossians 2:8).

"*¹⁸And many that believed came, and confessed, and shewed their deeds. ¹⁹Many of them also which used curious arts brought their books together, and burned them before all men: and they counted the price of them, and found it fifty thousand pieces of silver"* (Acts 19:18-19).

It is useless to be seeking after God when you know you have dealings with Satan. He cannot let you seek God. Unless you repent, confess and forsake your sins, and then renounce devil, burning all his properties, you cannot make any headway. But when you have confessed your sins, declare that Jesus is the Son of God and accept Him as your Savior. Your life receives transformation and you become a new person in the spirit. You cannot afford to miss this opportunity.

WHAT IS AN EVIL LOAD?

In simplest term, evil load is a generic term, which also means evil liability, which is beyond your power to pluck out of your life. Satan is the source of evil loads, and it takes the power and grace of God to throw away evil loads. However, evil loads can also be describe as -

- *Oppression; an arched device laid upon a victim to torment his life until death.*
- *A satanic restriction to achievements or limitation.*
- *Any demonic material that can bring visible or invisible problems into a person's life.*
- *A yoke that brings her victims under bondage or servitude.*
- *An instrument of agony.*
- *A plague of sickness, torment or affliction.*

It is nearly impossible to succeed when you are under the yoke of an evil load. Unless you discover the presence of any on time and do away with it through prayers, you cannot comfortably operate with success in anything you set out to achieve. This is because the purpose of evil loads is to stop your advancement, and if possible, destroy or ruin your destiny.

A perfect example of an evil load was clearly seen in the case of Samson and Delilah. Samson thought he had married a beautiful and lovely wife. But indeed, Delilah was a terrible evil load. We saw what happened. Samson was able to slaughter thousands of Philistine armies, but failing to destroy his evil load, it destroyed Samson.

What appears to be a small evil load can actually bring down a mighty man. Or influence him to take wrong and disheartening decisions. Evil loads have captured and wasted many people's lives and destinies. They have killed and buried many mighty men and women already. They have diverted so many people to reject good people and accept dangerous enemies as spouses.

Evil load can blind one's spiritual eyes; pup evil marks of hatred on such person. That's why many people experience a never-ending rejection wherever they go. When you fail to send evil loads back to their owners, they can shut your doors of success and opportunities forever. But such will not be your case in the name of Jesus.

> "*[16]They that see thee shall narrowly look upon thee, and consider thee, saying, Is this the man that made the earth to tremble, that did shake kingdoms; [17]That made the world as a wilderness, and destroyed the cities thereof; that opened not the house of his prisoners?*" (Isaiah 14:16-17)

> "*[2]And Pharaoh said, Who is the LORD, that I should obey his voice to let Israel go? I know not the LORD, neither will I let Israel go. [3]And they said, The God of the Hebrews hath met with us: let us go, we pray thee, three days' journey into the desert, and sacrifice unto the LORD our God; lest he fall upon us with pestilence, or with the sword. [4]And the king of Egypt said unto them, Wherefore do ye, Moses and Aaron, let the people from their works? Get you unto your burdens*" (Exodus 5:2-4).

A wise Christian would not want to live with any evil liability. Whatever that is capable of preventing you from making heaven is not worth keeping. That's why you have to do whatever that is possible to send evil loads back to senders, or at least, destroy them. Only then can you live a fulfilled life; a life that is free from evil riots, storms, failures, bad habits and struggles without success. Evil loads are capable of keeping people away from God's plan and promises. They bring disgrace, fear, indecision and curses upon people. Their mission is to kill and bury people. But when you confront evil loads through prayers, you are sure to win because God has already overcome the world in Christ Jesus for your sake. And your prosperity, life, marriage and family will remain secured in the grace of God through Christ Jesus.

> "*[29]And thou shalt grope at noonday, as the blind*

gropeth in darkness, and thou shalt not prosper in thy ways: and thou shalt be only oppressed and spoiled evermore, and no man shall save thee. ³⁰Thou shalt betroth a wife, and another man shall lie with her: thou shalt build a house, and thou shalt not dwell therein: thou shalt plant a vineyard, and shalt not gather the grapes thereof. ³¹Thine ox shall be slain before thine eyes, and thou shalt not eat thereof: thine ass shall be violently taken away from before thy face, and shall not be restored to thee: thy sheep shall be given unto thine enemies, and thou shalt have none to rescue them. ³²Thy sons and thy daughters shall be given unto another people, and thine eyes shall look, and fail with longing for them all the daylong: and there shall be no might in thine hand. ³³The fruit of thy land, and all thy labors, shall a nation which thou knowest not eat up; and thou shalt be only oppressed and crushed always" (Deuteronomy 28:29-33).

"³⁶The LORD shall bring thee, and thy king which thou shalt set over thee, unto a nation which neither thou nor thy fathers have known; and there shalt thou serve other gods, wood and stone. ³⁷And thou shalt become an astonishment, a proverb, and a byword, among all nations whither the LORD shall lead thee. ³⁸Thou shalt carry much seed out into the field, and shalt gather but little in; for the locust shall consume it. ³⁹Thou shalt plant vineyards, and dress them, but shalt neither drink of the wine, nor gather the grapes; for the worms shall eat them. ⁴⁰Thou shalt have olive trees throughout all thy coasts, but thou shalt not anoint thyself with the oil; for thine olive shall cast his fruit" (Deuteronomy 28:36-40).

It is good at this point to mention various types of evil loads you need to do away with at all cost in order to live a meaning and purposeful life on earth. They include personal, generational, family, tribal, traditional, environmental, inherited and national evil loads. None of these liabilities deserves to thrive in your life.

INSTANCES OF EVIL LOAD

Many couples failed in marriage because they failed to identity evil loads, which beset their marriage. There are some liabilities that when they plague your marriage, it will surely collapse in the cause of time. These kinds instigate divorces, separation and disheartening break ups. Equally, some specifically target businesses and academics. These evil loads are the source of infertility and sicknesses. See if you can identify any of these evil loads:

- *Evil appetite and lust for sexual satisfaction*
- *Load of impossibility*
- *Load of late marriage*
- *Load of poverty*
- *Load of demotion and rejection*
- *Load of none-achievement*
- *Load of memory failure and fear*
- *Load of disfavor*
- *Load of hardship*

HOW TO RETURN EVIL LOADS TO THEIR OWNERS

Here are few steps you can take to disown and dislodge any evil load that you identify operating in your life or that of your family. First, you have to realize that it would be humanly impossible to win spiritual battle, but possible with God. So, that means you have to bring God in to relieve you of all evil liabilities as you continue to trust in His mercy.

1. You have to be born-again. This is the first major step. You cannot avoid this step. *"Jesus answered and said unto him, Verily, verily, I say unto thee, Except a man be born-again, he cannot see the kingdom of God"* (John 3:3).

2. Repent and forsake your sins truly and thoroughly. You have to make up your mind on which side you want to be. Do you want to be on God's side or remain on devil's side? When you determine you want to come to God, you have to repent and forsake your sins in order to obtain mercy from God.

   "[13]He that covereth his sins shall not prosper: but whoso confesseth and forsaketh them shall have mercy" (Proverbs 28:13).

   "[3]And Samuel spake unto all the house of Israel, saying, If ye do return unto the LORD with all your hearts, then put away the strange gods and Ashtaroth from among you, and prepare your hearts unto the LORD, and serve him only: and he will deliver you out of the hand of the Philistines. [4]Then the children of Israel did put away Baalim and Ashtaroth, and served the LORD only" (1 Samuel 7:3-4).

3. You must have faith in God. You must be ready to trust in God and His mercy. This means that you have to start learning what it means to walk by faith and not by sight. You have to understand that God's ways are different from what you are accustomed to. So, whether what you

are seeing makes sense to you or not, do not believe it. Trust in God's mercy and have faith.

4. Pray aggressive until you get results. As you pray, be expectant that God will do a miracle for you. And like Jesus always said, you faith will heal and deliver you from all satanic loads and liabilities.

DESTINED TO OVERCOME

Every human that is born of a woman is engaged in one form of spiritual battle or another. The forces of darkness in this world contend with the forces of light and righteousness continually. And humans are caught up in the crossfire. But only true believers experience complete victory through Christ Jesus.

At the end of his ministry, Paul declared, *"⁷I have fought a good fight, I have finished my course, I have kept the faith"* (2 Timothy 4:7). He knew all along that he was fighting a spiritual warfare. What about you? Are you aware of your battles?

Many go through spiritual battles without being born-again. How do you expect to win? Battling the devil without being born-again cannot be a good fight. You cannot win. Unfortunately, majority of the people on earth are ignorant of the ongoing spiritual conflicts. They simply relate every battle going on in their lives to physical challenges. Such people are at the losing end. Regardless of how much wealth you can coordinate to solve every problem, you cannot win. Your battles will keep coming back in many other forms.

It is a wise thing to be conscious of the fact that everything that has physical dimension also has spiritual dimension. Most people on earth are under the bondage of one sin or another. You have to recognize that there is a demon behind every kind of sin. And such demons can only be addressed successfully through spiritual means, in this case prayer. The truth is that, if you are under the oppression of an evil spirit, you cannot reign over some circumstances even as a Christian.

> *"¹⁰And he was teaching in one of the synagogues on the Sabbath. ¹¹And, behold, there was a woman, which had a spirit of infirmity eighteen years, and was bowed together, and could in no wise lift up herself. ¹²And when Jesus saw her, he called her to him, and said unto her, Woman, thou art loosed from thine*

> *infirmity. ¹³And he laid his hands on her: and immediately she was made straight, and glorified God"* (Luke 13:10-13).

> *"¹⁶And ought not this woman, being a daughter of Abraham, whom Satan hath bound, lo, these eighteen years, be loosed from this bond on the Sabbath day?"* (Luke 13:16).

Let's take for instance, this woman that Satan bound for eighteen years. She was a true child of God, born-again and daughter of Abraham. Yet, Satan took her hostage for eighteen years. The source of her deliverance showed up but she was ignorant of Him. Satan tormented her with evil spirit of infirmity until Jesus said it was enough.

What is that sickness or disease in your life, which Jesus cannot bring to an end? Jesus is the deliverance that you have been praying and seeking for.

> *"³²And ye shall know the truth, and the truth shall make you free... ³⁶If the Son therefore shall make you free, ye shall be free indeed"* (John 8:32, 36).

Now that you have known the truth; that Jesus Christ, the Son of God, is the Lord and Savior of your life, you must act in faith at once, in order to be free from evil bondages. It also means that it is now time to resist the devil. If you are not born-again yet, do not waste any second more. Confess that Jesus is your Lord and Savior and receive Him in your heart today.

> *"³Jesus answered and said unto him, Verily, verily, I say unto thee, Except a man be born again, he can not see the kingdom of God"* (John 3:3).

> *"⁷Submit yourselves therefore to God. Resist the devil, and he will flee from you"* (James 4:7).

SPIRITUAL WARFARE

There is always a fight to fight and only those, who are born-again and know how to use God's Word has hope to have the victory. If you still have sin reigning inside of you, you are bound to die in your bondage. That is why being born-again is a necessity if you must succeed.

> "*^{23}But I see another law in my members, warring against the law of my mind, and bringing me into captivity to the law of sin which is in my members*" (Romans 7:23).

> "*^{12}For we wrestle not against flesh and blood, but against principalities, against powers, against the rulers of the darkness of this world, against spiritual wickedness in high places*" (Ephesians 6:12).

The battle within is more dangerous than the battle without. Sin is more destructive than the physical problem you are going through now. Your weak character and all acquired bad habits are worse than every physical problem you are going through now. Sin empowers every problem and makes the conflict fiercer. You may need to relocate your tent from Sodom and overcome your tempting Delilah so that through Jesus, you may receive access to healing and deliverance.

> "*^{10}And he was teaching in one of the synagogues on the Sabbath. ^{11}And, behold, there was a woman, which had a spirit of infirmity eighteen years, and was bowed together, and could in no wise lift up herself. ^{12}And when Jesus saw her, he called her to him, and said unto her, Woman, thou art loosed from thine infirmity. ^{13}And he laid his hands on her: and immediately she was made straight, and glorified God. ^{14}And the ruler of the synagogue answered with indignation, because that Jesus had healed on the Sabbath day, and said unto the people, There are six days in which men ought to work: in them therefore come and be healed, and not on the Sabbath day. ^{15}The Lord then answered him, and said, Thou hypocrite,*

doth not each one of you on the Sabbath loose his ox or his ass from the stall, and lead him away to watering? ¹⁶And ought not this woman, being a daughter of Abraham, whom Satan hath bound, lo, these eighteen years, be loosed from this bond on the Sabbath day?" (Luke 13:10-16)

It is of no use praying for physical healing, deliverance and prosperity if you are not ready to fight sin first.

"⁶Jesus saith unto him, I am the way, the truth, and the life: no man cometh unto the Father, but by me" (John 14:6).

Jesus said unto him, *"¹³He that covereth his sins shall not prosper: but whoso confesseth and forsaketh them shall have mercy"* (Proverbs 28:13).

The battle of life is sweet with assurance of victory if you are ready to repent, confess and forsake all your sins. You cannot stay outside your Father, Savior and in far country and fight your life's battle successfully. You need to come back to your source, creator and your God.

"¹⁷And when he came to himself, he said, How many hired servants of my father's have bread enough and to spare, and I perish with hunger! ¹⁸I will arise and go to my father, and will say unto him, Father, I have sinned against heaven, and before thee, ¹⁹And am no more worthy to be called thy son: make me as one of thy hired servants. ²⁰And he arose, and came to his father. But when he was yet a great way off, his father saw him, and had compassion, and ran, and fell on his neck, and kissed him. ²¹And the son said unto him, Father, I have sinned against heaven, and in thy sight, and am no more worthy to be called thy son. ²²But the father said to his servants, Bring forth the best robe, and put it on him; and put a ring on his hand, and shoes on his feet: ²³And bring hither the fatted calf, and kill it; and let us eat, and be merry: ²⁴For this my son was dead, and is alive again; he was lost, and is found. And they began to be merry" (Luke 15:17-24).

As a born again Christian, you can be sure of victory when you start praying. No matter how strong you are, how wealthy you are and how wise you are, you cannot win the battles of life without your Savior. Spiritual battles cannot be fought with human techniques. Being strong in occultism, witchcrafts and evil cannot give you true and lasting victory. You have to be strong in the Lord. You can only receive true answers to your prayers and full deliverance by fighting with God's amour.

> *"10Finally, my brethren, be strong in the Lord, and in the power of his might. 11Put on the whole armor of God that ye may be able to stand against the wiles of the devil. 12For we wrestle not against flesh and blood, but against principalities, against powers, against the rulers of the darkness of this world, against spiritual wickedness in high places"* (Ephesians 6:10-12).

Without the grace of God and the power of the Spirit of God, any of us will be as weak as the fallen giants. Experience has shown that minor problems can defeat those who lean on their human ability to fight the devil. No matter your experience, ability and maturity, if you don't lean on God and start praying, this problem will overcome you.

> *"28Hast thou not known? Hast thou not heard, that the everlasting God, the LORD, the Creator of the ends of the earth, fainteth not, neither is weary? there is no searching of his understanding. 29He giveth power to the faint; and to them that have no might he increaseth strength. 30Even the youths shall faint and be weary, and the young men shall utterly fall: 31But they that wait upon the LORD shall renew their strength; they shall mount up with wings as eagles; they shall run, and not be weary; and they shall walk, and not faint"* (Isaiah 40:28-31).

If you need to fast, don't delay, if you need to pray for many nights, wake up to pray until your deliverance comes true. Let your greatest concern be to win and receive full deliverance. People, who overcome, are known for their resilience in prayer, vigilance, faith and resistance until the end. As a true child of God, you are destined to overcome every problem including the present ones in the name of Jesus.

PROVISION, PROMISE AND VICTORY

God has made adequate provision and has given precious promises by which every believer can receive and enjoy the best of life on earth. Christ suffered and died for this purpose. You can obtain every good thing promised by God by recognizing the need in your life.

> "⁹And Jabez was more honorable than his brethren: and his mother called his name Jabez, saying, Because I bare him with sorrow. ¹⁰And Jabez called on the God of Israel, saying, Oh that thou wouldest bless me indeed, and enlarge my coast, and that thine hand might be with me, and that thou wouldest keep me from evil, that it may not grieve me! And God granted him that which he requested" (1 Chronicles 4:9-10).

> "¹¹For the LORD God is a sun and shield: the LORD will give grace and glory: no good thing will he withhold from them that walk uprightly" (Psalms 84:11).

Jabez recognized the need for change, blessing and deliverance from all evil in his life. He became thirsty for change. The thirst and hunger led him into action. He wholeheartedly consecrated his life to God, holding back nothing and God never disappointed him.

> "²²And all things, whatsoever ye shall ask in prayer, believing, ye shall receive" (Matthew 21:22).

> "³According as his divine power hath given unto us all things that pertain unto life and godliness, through the knowledge of him that hath called us to glory and virtue: ⁴Whereby are given unto us exceeding great and precious promises: that by these ye might be partakers of the divine nature, having escaped the corruption that is in the world through lust" (2 Peter 1:3-4).

If you have faith in God's promise, and pray, claim his promises, He will not say no. There are many great and precious promises waiting for you to be claimed in this program. It is not enough for you to know what God has promised you through his word. You have to fight every power that will try to stop you from enjoying them. No matter how long it takes you have to persist until all the oppressors' bows. Through consistent Christian life, prayer and even fasting, you must insist until you receive and enjoy all that Christ has provided for you through God's promise.

> "*⁶Be careful for nothing; but in every thing by prayer and supplication with thanksgiving let your requests be made known unto God*" (Philippians 4:6).

You must not be afraid of asking God for anything He has promised you in His words. The grace of God is sufficient to help you get every good thing no matter the economic situation of the world or the failures of the men of science. If the word of God promised you healing, deliverance and prosperity, believe it.

> "*⁷And the LORD appeared unto Abram, and said, Unto thy seed will I give this land: and there builded he an altar unto the LORD, who appeared unto him*" (Genesis 12:7).

> "*¹⁵For all the land which thou seest, to thee will I give it, and to thy seed forever*" (Genesis 13:15).

> "*⁷And I will establish my covenant between me and thee and thy seed after thee in their generations for an everlasting covenant, to be a God unto thee, and to thy seed after thee. ⁸And I will give unto thee, and to thy seed after thee, the land wherein thou art a stranger, all the land of Canaan, for an everlasting possession; and I will be their God*" (Genesis 17:7-8).

Abraham and his seeds were outside the land of Canaan when God promised to give them the land as an inheritance. He saw the land and God promised to give them the land forever. At the age of ninety-nine years, God re-emphasized

His promise to Abraham and promised to fulfill it. That's why you should trust God when He has promised you healing, deliverance, prosperity and child bearing, no matter how old you are or how long it takes. As long as you believe God, no matter the circumstance, you will receive an answer. The land promised to Abraham, and his seed was in the hands of Israel's worst enemies at the time Israel left Egypt.

> "^{16}And it came to pass, as we went to prayer, a certain damsel possessed with a spirit of divination met us, which brought her masters much gain by soothsaying: ^{17}The same followed Paul and us, and cried, saying, These men are the servants of the most high God, which shew unto us the way of salvation. ^{18}And this did she many days. But Paul, being grieved, turned and said to the spirit, I command thee in the name of Jesus Christ to come out of her. And he came out the same hour. ^{19}And when her masters saw that the hope of their gains was gone, they caught Paul and Silas, and drew them into the marketplace unto the rulers" (Acts 16:16-19).

The witches and wizards, occult grand masters may have swallowed your destiny. They may be making gains through your brain, womb or any part of your organs in their covens and altars. Hannah was once a barren woman. Her womb was shut up and her adversary provoked her, insulted her. The womb of everything you do on earth may be shut up. She wept day and night, year after year until she found God's promise.

Have you been surrounded by witches and wizards? I want to remind you that the same thing happened to Elijah until he went into prayers. Allies of power enemies once surrounded Jehoshaphat and he went to God. Daniel's colleagues hated him with great passion and set him up to be eaten by hungry lions. Peter was once locked up in prison. So, no matter what you are going through, great people of God have suffered worst things. The good news is that there is a promise for your deliverance. God has made provision for your complete freedom through His Word.

"³²And ye shall know the truth, and the truth shall make you free. ³³They answered him, We be Abraham's seed, and were never in bondage to any man: how sayest thou, Ye shall be made free? ³⁴Jesus answered them, Verily, verily, I say unto you, Whosoever committeth sin is the servant of sin. ³⁵And the servant abideth not in the house forever: but the Son abideth ever. ³⁶If the Son therefore shall make you free, ye shall be free indeed"(John 8:32-36).

They answered him, "We be Abraham's seed, and were never in bondage to any man: how sayest thou, ye shall be made free? Jesus answered them, verily, verily, I say unto you, whosoever, committed sin is the servant of sin. And the servant abideth not in the house forever but the son abideth ever. If the son shall therefore make you free, ye shall be free indeed."

Goliath was determined to finish the children of Israel. You may have a Goliath in your place of work, family, your body as sickness, God has promised to deliver you. Pharaoh vowed to keep the children of Israel in bondage for life but they have a promise covering their deliverance from every enemy. No enemy has the right to keep you too long if you are born again. The red sea was determined not to give way to the children of Israel. They were cut off from God's promises, provisions and inheritance. God delivered them from Egypt, divided their Red sea because of his promise. The entire first born of Egypt died at mid night for their sake. No problem or power can keep you under bondage forever. If only you can pray, your enemies will bow in this program. You will experience a Passover and a move to another level of life.

"⁶The LORD our God spake unto us in Horeb, saying, Ye have dwelt long enough in this mount: ⁷Turn you, and take your journey, and go to the mount of the Amorites, and unto all the places nigh thereunto, in the plain, in the hills, and in the vale, and in the south, and by the sea side, to the land of the Canaanites, and unto Lebanon, unto the great river, the river Euphrates. ⁸Behold, I have set the land before you: go

> *in and possess the land which the LORD sware unto your fathers, Abraham, Isaac, and Jacob, to give unto them and to their seed after them"* (Deuteronomy 1:6-8).

> *"³⁵And the same day, when the even was come, he saith unto them, Let us pass over unto the other side"* (Mark 4:35).

It is not God's will for you to remain in bondage, problem or one level of life too long. This prayer program will take you into a journey of freedom. You need to re-possess your health, wealth, etc. You may have been suffering in the wilderness with all manner of lack, poverty and death of all kind. God can provide in the desert and renew a life that is about to give up the ghost.

> *"¹⁷And God heard the voice of the lad; and the angel of God called to Hagar out of heaven, and said unto her, What aileth thee, Hagar? fear not; for God hath heard the voice of the lad where he is. ¹⁸Arise, lift up the lad, and hold him in thine hand; for I will make him a great nation. ¹⁹And God opened her eyes, and she saw a well of water; and she went, and filled the bottle with water, and gave the lad drink"* (Genesis 21:17-19).

You may be abandoned; deceived by loved ones to die but if you can pray in this program, God will deliver you. You may be spiritually blind; God will open your eye to see abundant prosperity. You will be linked up to divine wealth. But you need to believe in God's promises and provisions. In the wilderness, the children of Israel met bitter water but when they cried unto God their waters was made sweet.

> *"²³And when they came to Marah, they could not drink of the waters of Marah, for they were bitter: therefore the name of it was called Marah. ²⁴And the people murmured against Moses, saying, What shall we drink? ²⁵And he cried unto the LORD; and the LORD shewed him a tree, which when he had cast into the waters, the waters were made sweet: there he made for them a statute and an ordinance, and there he*

proved them" (Exodus 15:23-25).

Your life may not be better now but God will turn your water into sweet honey.

DIVINE PROVISION

If you need deliverance, God will provide for you. If you need healing, your healing will come. The wall of Jericho may be standing before you. All your enemies may have vowed never to let you go. Your life may be full of sorrow, bitterness, confusion, lack, sickness and diseases, if you believe God's provision, all your enemies must bow. The Amorites believed that the land of Canaan was their ancestral home. They vowed never to vacate the land of promise. They were determined to resist any attempt by Israel to enter their promised land. The children of Israel based their claim on God's promises and provision. They were determined to possess the land despite all oppositions on their way. In the face of all oppositions, God reassured the children of Israel and stated again his covenant promise and provision of the land. (*See* Deuteronomy 30:1-10)

If God promised you anything, believe him because He is faithful to fulfill all his promises.

> *"And the LORD gave unto Israel all the land which he sware to give unto their fathers; and they possessed it, and dwelt therein. And the LORD gave them rest round about, according to all that he sware unto their fathers: and there stood not a man of all their enemies before them; the LORD delivered all their enemies into their hand. There failed not ought of any good thing which the LORD had spoken unto the house of Israel; all came to pass"* (Joshua 21:43-45).

Not even death, the devil can stand against God's word. His promises are yea and Amen. If you will remain faithful to his promises, he will provide for you and deliver you until your life will be freed from all enemies.

God is faithful to fulfill all his promises.

> *"Then the children of Judah came unto Joshua in Gilgal: and Caleb the son of Jephunneh the Kenezite said unto him, Thou knowest the thing that the LORD said unto Moses the man of God concerning me and*

thee in Kadeshbarnea. Forty years old was I when Moses the servant of the LORD sent me from Kadeshbarnea to espy out the land; and I brought him word again as it was in mine heart. Nevertheless my brethren that went up with me made the heart of the people melt: but I wholly followed the LORD my God. And Moses sware on that day, saying, Surely the land whereon thy feet have trodden shall be thine inheritance, and thy children's for ever, because thou hast wholly followed the LORD my God. And now, behold, the LORD hath kept me alive, as he said, these forty and five years, even since the LORD spake this word unto Moses, while the children of Israel wandered in the wilderness: and now, lo, I am this day fourscore and five years old. As yet I am as strong this day as I was in the day that Moses sent me: as my strength was then, even so is my strength now, for war, both to go out, and to come in. Now therefore give me this mountain, whereof the LORD spake in that day; for thou heardest in that day how the Anakims were there, and that the cities were great and fenced: if so be the LORD will be with me, then I shall be able to drive them out, as the LORD said. And Joshua blessed him, and gave unto Caleb the son of Jephunneh Hebron for an inheritance" (Joshua 14:6-13).

God made promise to Caleb and after forty years, he was kept alive to receive the fulfillments. He came to the land that God promised to give him. He did not inherit or possessed his possession until he asked. If you don't asked, you will not receive what God has provided for you. God anointed David but Saul refused to allow him rule. God promised to save him from all his enemies but he has to pray in times of danger. His enemies fought him daily, oppressed him frequently, trying to swallow him up. They twisted his word conspired against him but he put his confidence in God.

"What time I am afraid, I will trust in thee. In God I will praise his word, in God I have put my trust; I will not fear what flesh can do unto me…

> Thou tellest my wanderings: put thou my tears into thy bottle: *are they* not in thy book?" (Psalms 56:3-4, 8).

> *"In God will I praise His Word: in the LORD will I praise his Word. In God have I put my trust: I will not be afraid what man can do unto me"* (Psalms 56:10-11).

When there is a promise, wise people pray but the unwise postpone their prayer till the master of the house has risen up and shut the door before they start knocking.

> *"Strive to enter in at the strait gate: for many, I say unto you, will seek to enter in, and shall not be able. When once the master of the house is risen up, and hath shut to the door, and ye begin to stand without, and to knock at the door, saying, Lord, Lord, open unto us; and he shall answer and say unto you, I know you not whence ye are: Then shall ye begin to say, We have eaten and drunk in thy presence, and thou hast taught in our streets. But he shall say, I tell you, I know you not whence ye are; depart from me, all ye workers of iniquity. There shall be weeping and gnashing of teeth, when ye shall see Abraham, and Isaac, and Jacob, and all the prophets, in the kingdom of God, and you yourselves thrust out"* (Luke 13:24-28).

We are all in battle and our triumph or defeat is dependent in our attitude at the hour of battle. Believers are to seek for God's mercy in times of trials (Psalms 136:1-26). After our salvation, we must give prayers first place early every morning and at all times until the enemies bows. Your prayers must be in faith believing God for impossibilities. Believers should trust God and believe God because their tears are preserved in God's bottles. Our cries to God cannot be in vain.

> *"And he said unto Jesus, Lord, remember me when thou comest into thy kingdom"* (Luke 23:42).

> *"And he said, let me go, for the day breaketh. And he said, I will not let thee go, except thou bless me"* (Genesis 32:26).

You must cry for salvation, for help, deliverance and change. David faced great problems but the promise of God kept him until he fulfilled his destiny.

> *"For David, after he had served his own generation by the will of God, fell on sleep, and was laid unto his fathers, and saw corruption"* (Acts 13:36).

You must not accept defeat, any problem until you fulfill your destiny and make it to heaven.

GOD PROMISE, POWER AND VICTORY

Paul described our problems on earth as light afflictions, which cannot and supposed not to destroy a true child of God.

> *"Again, think ye that we excuse ourselves unto you? we speak before God in Christ: but we do all things, dearly beloved, for your edifying"* (2 Corinthians 12:19).

> *"For, behold, the Lord, the LORD of hosts, doth take away from Jerusalem and from Judah the stay and the staff, the whole stay of bread, and the whole stay of water, The mighty man, and the man of war, the judge, and the prophet, and the prudent, and the ancient"* (Isaiah 3:1-2).

As long as you are here on earth trying to do the right thing, the witches and wizards who believe that the earth is their territory will be energized by the spirit of the age to fire strange arrows into your life. They may attack you with the fires of sickness, poverty, deception, slander, conspiracy, division, contention, strife, criticism and betrayer. It may be a fire of persecution, affliction, oppression, slavery, tribulations, trail, injustice and denial of fundamental human rights, whatever you are going through now; there is a promise of a higher power to stop it. If your problem is coming from the powers in the waters, God promised to be with you, it will not overflow you. If it is from the fire, the promise say, it will not burn you (*See* Daniel 3:19-30).

Not even satanic flames shall be allowed to destroy you in vain. Though affliction may come from all sides, but God's promise will continue to stand greater than any affliction. The Lord will deliver you from them all. A day is coming, during or after this program when you will look for your problems and will not see any trace of them.

God's promises and His power of deliverance are the inheritance of all believers.

> *"And the Lord shall deliver me from every evil work, and will preserve me unto his heavenly kingdom: to whom be glory for ever and ever. Amen"* (2 Timothy 4:18).
>
> *"There hath no temptation taken you but such as is common to man: but God is faithful, who will not suffer you to be tempted above that ye are able; but will with the temptation also make a way to escape, that ye may be able to bear it"* (1 Corinthians 10:13).

God never leaves us alone to fight against the tempter and his temptations in our natural strength. He promised to help us and deliver us from every evil works, to preserve us unto his heavenly kingdom. He promised not to allow us to suffer from any temptation that is above us. Whatever you are going through now is under God's power. There is a promise of victory attached to every problem in the life of a believer. What you need to do is to be a believer before you start praying. As you resist the devil, your problems in this program, the sustaining grace of God will appear for your deliverance.

> *"For in that he himself hath suffered being tempted, he is able to succour them that are tempted"* (Hebrews 2:18).
>
> *"Neither is there any creature that is not manifest in his sight: but all things are naked and opened unto the eyes of him with whom we have to do. Seeing then that we have a great high priest that is passed into the heavens, Jesus the Son of God, let us hold fast our profession. For we have not an high priest which cannot be touched with the feeling of our infirmities; but was in all points tempted like as we are, yet without sin. Let us therefore come boldly unto the throne of grace, that we may obtain mercy, and find grace to help in time of need"* (Hebrews 4:13-16).

Jesus has passed through every trials and he is able to deliver anyone in trouble from whatsoever trouble. Once you start praying as you repent, confess and forsake your sins, your enemies will be disgraced. Prayers of believers bring Jesus into the battlefield of our life. Without His presence, we cannot walk at liberty without being harmed, defeated by the wicked spirit and evil people on earth. When the enemy touches us, Jesus is touched, when there is storm we need to awake Christ through prayers.

> *"Finally, brethren, whatsoever things are true, whatsoever things are honest, whatsoever things are just, whatsoever things are pure, whatsoever things are lovely, whatsoever things are of good report; if there be any virtue, and if there be any praise, think on these things"* (Philippians 4:8).

To attract deliverance into your life now, seek for truth, honest life, live just, pure with love. Do things that will bring good report and praise to the name of God. Resist the devils temptations, separate from tempters and temptresses, close every evil channel through which the temptation is coming and pray for God's keeping power and sustaining grace. Your victory is sure as you obey God's word and pray the prayer in this book.

GENERAL PRAYERS

You can pray these general prayers as many times as possible. These prayer points focus on expanding your blessings; attracting new blessings and purging your problems. I believe that as you pray, your prayers will give birth to new things, open your heavens and attract divine unmerited favor until all your enemy bows.

> *"And I will stretch out my hand, and smite Egypt with all my wonders which I will do in the midst thereof: and after that he will let you go"* (Exodus 3:20).

> *"Not because I desire a gift: but I desire fruit that may abound to your account. But I have all, and abound: I am full, having received of Epaphroditus the things which were sent from you, an odor of a sweet smell, a sacrifice acceptable, well pleasing to God. But my God shall supply all your need according to his riches in glory by Christ Jesus"* (Philippians 4:17-19).

> *"For the LORD God is a sun and shield: the LORD will give grace and glory: no good thing will he withhold from them that walk uprightly"* (Psalms 84:11).

In few hours from now, as you pray the prayers below, your level will change and you can never remain the same.

PRAYER POINTS

1. Owners of evil loads in my life, appear, carry your loads, in the name of Jesus.

2. Blood of Jesus, flow into my life and deliver me from every evil load, in the name of Jesus.

3. I command every evil load in my life to drop by force, in the name of Jesus.

4. Fire of God, burn to ashes every evil load in my life, in the name of Jesus.

5. Any invisible hand stealing from my life, I cut you off by force, in the name of Jesus.

6. Every enemy of my deliverance, be exposed and be disgraced, in the name of Jesus.

7. Blood of Jesus, speak me out of every trouble, in the name of Jesus.

8. Any evil personality attacking my life in my dreams, be disgraced forever, in the name of Jesus.

9. Any evil thing that has married me, you are wicked, die, in the name of Jesus.

10. Any evil personality controlling my life, I cut off your existence, in the name of Jesus.

11. Every problem in my life, gather yourself together and die, in the name of Jesus.

12. Every hidden enemy of my life, be exposed and be disgraced, in the name of Jesus.

13. Any mountain of problem standing between my greatness and I, disappear forever, in the name of Jesus.

14. Any power postponing my deliverance, wherever you are, die, in the name of Jesus.

15. Every problem that has woken up with me this morning, you will not go to bed with me, die now, in the name of Jesus.

16. I command every organ of my body to receive full deliverance, in the name of Jesus. *Job 22:28*

17. Any evil eye monitoring my destiny, be blinded, in the name of Jesus.

18. Blood of Jesus, quench every strange fire burning in my life, in the name of Jesus.

19. Any evil movement all over the world against my life, be demobilized, in the name of Jesus.

20. Every book, satanic files, against my life, catch fire, burn to ashes, in the name of Jesus.

21. I recover double every good thing I had ever lost in life, in the name of Jesus.

22. Every stubborn enemy in the battlefield of my life, what are you still doing, die, in the name of Jesus.

23. Every evil support against my life, be withdrawn by force, in the name of Jesus.

24. Blood of Jesus, flow into my life and destroy my captivity, in the name of Jesus.

25. Every yoke of bondage in my life, break to pieces, in the name of Jesus.

26. Let the backbone of my enemy begin to break by force, in the name of Jesus.

27. O Lord, arise and take me away from devils camp, in the name of Jesus.

28. Every dream of defeats in my life, be converted to victory, in the name of Jesus.

29. I lift every satanic embargo placed against my life, in the name of Jesus.

30. Any evil leg that has ever walked into my life, walk out, in the name of Jesus.

31. Any power that is reviving my problems, be disgraced unto death, in the name of Jesus.

32. Every arrow of shame, disgrace and reproach in my life, backfire, in the name of Jesus.

33. Fire of God, burn to ashes every disease germ in my life, in the name of Jesus.

34. Every enemy of my deliverance, you are finished, die by fire, in the name of Jesus.

35. Any battle going on against my life, end to my favor, in the name of Jesus.

36. Let every dark thing in my life disappear by force, in the name of Jesus.

37. Any witchcraft animal living inside me, die, in the name of Jesus.

38. Any evil program going on against my life, be terminated, in the name of Jesus.

39. Every weakness in my life, be converted to strength, in the name of Jesus.

40. I walk out from the camp of the defeated ones, in the name of Jesus.

41. Any evil king or queen sitting upon my inheritance, be unseated by death, in the name of Jesus.

42. Any evil personality living inside me, come out and die, in the name of Jesus.

43. Any demon on suicide mission against my life, come out, die alone, in the name of Jesus.

44. I command the earth to open and swallow my problems, in the name of Jesus.

45. Any serpent in the garden of my life, come out and die, in the name of Jesus.

46. Every enemy of my peace, victory on earth, receive destructions, in the name of Jesus.

47. I terminate the life of my problems, in the name of Jesus.

48. Every weapon of the enemy against my life, be destroyed, in the name of Jesus.

49. I command my enemies to make mistakes that will favor me, in the name of Jesus.

50. Every enemy of my promotion and deliverance, be disgraced, in the name of Jesus.

51. Any witch or wizard that has vowed to waste my life, be wasted, in the name of Jesus.

52. Let the earthquake and let my deliverance appear by force, in the name of Jesus.

53. Let darkness in any area of my life disappear, in the name of Jesus.

54. Any power contending with my joy and peace, die, in the name of Jesus.

55. O Lord, arise and re-organize my life to your glory, in the name of Jesus.

56. Any power attacking my handwork, receive double destruction, in the name of Jesus.

57. Let every damage my life has ever suffered receive divine repair, in the name of Jesus.

58. I recover double every opportunity I have ever lost, in the name of Jesus.

59. I command all the supporters of my problems to withdraw by force, in the name of Jesus.

60. Any power expanding my problems, die without delay, in the name of Jesus.

61. Any power that has arrested my progress, release it now, in the name of Jesus.

62. Every work of the devil in my life, be terminated, in the name of Jesus.

63. O Lord, arise and deliver my hijacked destiny, in the name of Jesus.

64. Let the powers that activate evil work fail in my life, in the name of Jesus.

65. I command my diverted progress to come back by force, in the name of Jesus.

66. Let all satanic angels contending with my destiny be disgraced, in the name of Jesus.

67. I break and loose myself from every satanic curse and covenants, in the name of Jesus.

68. Any witchcraft property in my life, catch fire, burn to ashes, in the name of Jesus.

69. I command every promise of God to manifest in my life, in the name of Jesus.

70. I reject every evil prophecy and visions in my life, in the name of Jesus.

71. I command my life to move forward by fire, in the name of Jesus.

72. Any satanic traffic warder standing against me, die, in the name of Jesus.

73. Every unprofitable load in my life, drop by force, in the name of Jesus.

74. You my personal stronghold, collapse by thunder in the name of Jesus.

75. Any shame distributor assigned against my life, die with your shame, in the name of Jesus.

76. Blood of Jesus, speak me out of every trouble, in the name of Jesus.

77. Any arrow of infirmity fired into any area of my life, backfire, in the name of Jesus.

78. Every demon of late progress in my life, I cast you out, in the name of Jesus.

79. Let every oppressor in my life be oppressed unto death, in the name of Jesus.

80. Any satanic prayer going on against me, back fire, in the name of Jesus.

81. I scatter unto shame every satanic re-enforcement against me, in the name of Jesus.

82. Let the helpers of my enemies be manipulated to my favor, in the name of Jesus.

83. Let the strength of my enemies be broken to pieces, in the name of Jesus.

84. You my problems, receive double destruction, in the name of Jesus.

85. Let the brain of all the powers behind my problem receive confusion forever, in the name of Jesus.

86. O Lord, empower me with explosive breakthroughs, in the name of Jesus.

87. Every seed of sin in my life, die, in the name of Jesus.

88. Blood of Jesus, repurchase me from every disease's captivity, in the name of Jesus.

89. Let the power of God break every spiritual prison and deliver me, in the name of Jesus.

90. Any evil movement in my body, stop and die, in the name of Jesus.

91. Any power postponing my healing and deliverance, die, in the name of Jesus.

92. Any strange fire, traveling in my body, be quenched, in the name of Jesus.

93. Blood of Jesus, speak death unto every infirmity in my body, in the name of Jesus.

94. Every enemy of my healing and deliverance, die, in the name of Jesus.

95. Let the pillar of witchcraft in my life be uprooted, in the name of Jesus.

96. Every satanic embargo placed against my healing, be lifted, in the name of Jesus.

97. Any evil sacrifice offered against my healing; expire, in the name of Jesus.

98. Any power attacking my health in the dream, die, in the name of Jesus.

99. Any evil covenant hindering my healing, break, in the name of Jesus.

100. I break and loose myself from every curse against my destiny, in the name of Jesus.

101. Holy Ghost fire, burn to ashes every disease germ in my body, in the name of Jesus.

102. Any organ of my life, captured by sickness and disease, be released, in the name of Jesus.

103. Any power defiling my beauty, die by force, in the name of Jesus.

104. I command all the powers behind my suffering to die, in the name of Jesus.

105. Every messenger of pains in my body, carry your message, in the name of Jesus.

106. I break the backbone of every problem in my life, in the name of Jesus.

107. Every demonic wound in any area of my life, receive healing, in the name of Jesus.

108. I shake off every sickness in my body, in the name of Jesus.

You my head, body, soul and spirit, discharge every problem in you, in the name of Jesus.

Chapter 2

WARFARE PRAYERS SECTION

CHAPTER OVERVIEW

Prayers in this section include prayers for financial assistance, finance breakthrough, financial miracles, divine breakthrough, divine opportunities, divine connections, business breakthrough, divine promotion, prosperity, protection from enemies, protection from evil, deliverance from poverty, overcoming enemies in the place of work, paying bills, prospering in business, divine connections, prospering in foreign land, recovering lost businesses, recovering a lost job, recovering all your loss, reviving collapsed or collapsing business, revoking evil decrees, rise from defeat, searching and finding jobs, stopping determined enemies, succeeding where others are failing, survive economic meltdown/famine.

PRAYER TOPICS ON THIS SECTION

1. Prayer for financial assistance — 41
2. Prayer for financial breakthrough — 45
3. Prayer for financial miracles — 49
4. Prayer for divine breakthrough — 53
5. Prayer for divine opportunities — 56
6. Prayer for divine connections — 60
7. Prayer for business breakthrough — 66
8. Prayer for divine promotion — 70
9. Prayer for prosperity — 74
10. Prayer for protection from enemies — 77
11. Prayer for protection from evil — 81
12. Prayer deliverance from poverty — 85
13. Prayer to overcome enemies in the place of work — 89
14. Prayer to pay bills — 93
15. Prayer to prosper in business — 97
16. Prayer for divine connections — 101
17. Prayer to prosper in foreign land — 109
18. Prayer to recover lost businesses — 116
19. Prayer to recover a lost job — 120
20. Prayer to recover all your loss — 124
21. Prayer to revive collapsed or collapsing business — 128
22. Prayer to revoke evil decrees — 133
23. Prayer to rise from defeat — 137
24. Prayer to search and find a job — 141
25. Prayer to stop determined enemies — 145
26. Prayer to succeed where others are failing — 149
27. Prayer to survive famine and economic meltdown — 153

PRAYER FOR FINANCIAL ASSISTANCE

It is very important to determine first in your heart to help others with what you already have, before you could expect to receive from God and men. It is always hard to receive without giving. You can utilize your finances profitably, expecting eternal rewards, when you use most of it to help the poor and spread the gospel.

> "I have shewed you all things, how that so laboring ye ought to support the weak, and to remember the words of the Lord Jesus, how he said, It is more blessed to give than to receive" (Acts 20:35).

> "For God so loved the world, that he gave his only begotten Son, that whosoever believeth in him should not perish, but have everlasting life" (John 3:16).

> "Jesus answered and said unto her, If thou knewest the gift of God, and who it is that saith to thee, Give me to drink; thou wouldest have asked of him, and he would have given thee living water" (John 4:10).

The best kind of giving is a giving to connects people to God's grace and mercy; when it becomes evident to the beneficiary that it was not an act of man, but God. If you desire unlimited financial help from God and men, then use what you have to help people to experience grace and mercies of God.

The biggest charity donation ever recorded in history was when 40 American billionaires pledged to give at least half of their money to good causes. Notice also that when your gift helps the beneficiary temporarily, but kills soul and spirit, you have given wrongly. In conclusion, without salvation, that is being born-again, man at his best state, with all his gifts, are altogether useless.

"LORD, make me to know mine end, and the measure of my days, what it is; that I may know how frail I am. Behold, thou hast made my days as an handbreadth; and mine age is as nothing before thee: verily every man at his best state is altogether vanity. Selah. Surely every man walketh in a vain shew: surely they are disquieted in vain: he heapeth up riches, and knoweth not who shall gather them" (Psalms 39:4-6).

If you desire financial help, as you spend time in prayers, determine in your heart to invest in helping people experience the goodness and mercies of God. I believe prayers in this section will go a long way in promoting you financially.

July 17, 15

PRAYER POINTS

1. O Lord, send financial help and helpers to me from above, in the name of Jesus.

2. Power to withdraw from heaven's bank, possess me now, in the name of Jesus.

3. O Lord, deliver me from poverty by Your power, in the name of Jesus.

4. Any evil personality, sitting upon my finances, be unseated, in the name of Jesus.

5. I walk into abundant financial realm by God's leading, in the name of Jesus.

6. You, my financial helpers, begin to locate me by force, in the name of Jesus.

7. Let the angels of my blessings locate me by force, in the name of Jesus.

8. You, my open-heaven for financial success, rain down wealth by force, in the name of Jesus.

9. Every satanic bank keeping my finance, release it now and collapse, in the name of Jesus.

10. Any strongman that is blocking my financial helper, fall down and die, in the name of Jesus.

11. O Lord, lead me into a business that will prosper me financially, in the name of Jesus.

12. Every financial hindrance on my way, clear away by force, in the name of Jesus.

13. Any witchcraft animal that has swallowed my finances, vomit it, in the name of Jesus.

14. From today onwards, I will begin to meet people, who will help me financially, in the name of Jesus.

15. O Lord, grant me financial help by Your power, in the name of Jesus.

16. Let my heaven open for financial breakthrough forever and ever, in the name of Jesus.

17. Father Lord, embrace me with financial success like never before on earth, in the name of Jesus.

18. Anointing to prosper financially, possess me completely, in the name of Jesus.

PRAYER FOR FINANCIAL BREAKTHROUGH

When you discover that unclean spirit of excessive love of money possesses you, bow your knees and start praying for immediate deliverance. You cannot be possessed by the spirit of mammon and expect God to release your financial breakthrough. Scriptures revealed that when money is in the hands of the wicked and selfish people, the world suffers. That's why God cannot allow His true wealth to rest in the hands of the wicked. Deal with the spirit of mammon first.

> "⁷For we brought nothing into this world, and it is certain we can carry no thing out. ⁸And having food and raiment let us be therewith content. ⁹But they that will be rich fall into temptation and a snare, and into many foolish and hurtful lusts, which drown men in destruction and perdition. ¹⁰For the love of money is the root of all evil: which while some coveted after, they have erred from the faith, and pierced themselves through with many sorrows" (1 Timothy 6:7-10).

As a matter of fact, it is a great punishment to be under the control and influence of mammon. This is when, even with all the monies in the world in your possession, you cannot be satisfied and cannot enjoy rest and peace. Sandy Weill, the man who created Citi Group, Larry Ellison, founder of the software giant oracle, and Pierre Omidyar, founder of eBay, are among the billionaires who made a public pledge to give away more than half their fortune. They understand that mammon cannot give rest and peace, that's why they have to give all the money away.

> "³⁸Give, and it shall be given unto you; good measure, pressed down, and shaken together, and running over, shall men give into your bosom. For with the same measure that ye mete withal it shall be measured to you again" (Luke 6:38).

"¹And he looked up, and saw the rich men casting their gifts into the treasury. ²And he saw also a certain poor widow casting in thither two mites. ³And he said, Of a truth I say unto you, that this poor widow hath cast in more than they all: ⁴For all these have of their abundance cast in unto the offerings of God: but she of her penury hath cast in all the living that she had" (Luke 21:1-4).

Yet the world still suffers because of shortage of true givers. God created all things, including all that the entire people on earth require to succeed and be comfortable. But as long as earth's wealth is in the hands of a few stingy people, the world will continue to be a place of torment and people continue to suffer.

Sat July 18, 15
Mon Oct 9, 2017

PRAYER POINTS

1. Father Lord, deliver me from financial predicaments, in the name of Jesus.

2. You, my deeply rooted financial problem, be uprooted by fire, in the name of Jesus.

3. Every bondage of financial lack and debt in my life, die, in the name of Jesus.

4. Blood of Jesus, place me into financial prosperity, *Now* in the name of Jesus.

5. My angel of blessing for financial breakthrough, locate me now, in the name of Jesus.

6. Let my financial problem provoke angelic assistance, in the name of Jesus.

7. Every satanic blockage against my finances, be dismantled, in the name of Jesus. *Now*

8. Any power from the waters that has swallowed my finance, vomit it, in the name of Jesus.

9. Let the mighty hand of God release finances into my account, in the name of Jesus. *(Bank, 401, Annuity, Real Estate Accounts)*

10. Any problem that is attacking my finance, die by force, in the name of Jesus.

11. Any devourer of my finances, die by force, in the name of Jesus.

12. Every hunter of my finances, be disgraced in shame, in the name of Jesus.

13. I anchor my business to financial prosperity, in the name of Jesus.

14. Let the bank of heaven release divine finances into my business, in the name of Jesus.

15. Any dead area of my finance, receive resurrection power, in the name of Jesus.

16. O Lord, bless me financially with a dumbfounding miracle, in the name of Jesus.

17. Every embargo on my financial progress, be lifted, in the name of Jesus.

18. I destroy every restriction placed on my finances, in the name of Jesus

19. O Lord, provide the finances I needed to achieve greater things on earth, in the name of Jesus.

20. I receive power from God to prosper financially, in the name of Jesus.

PRAYER FOR FINANCIAL MIRACLES

Isn't it wiser to first establish what to do with finance before praying for financial miracles? When your thinking is right, God is able to bless you abundantly through this program. The state of your mind is critical because God sees your heart and all its intents.

> "²Beloved, I wish above all things that thou mayest prosper and be in health, even as thy soul prospereth" (3 John 1:2).

> "⁹And Jabez was more honorable than his brethren: and his mother called his name Jabez, saying, Because I bare him with sorrow. ¹⁰And Jabez called on the God of Israel, saying, Oh that thou wouldest bless me indeed, and enlarge my coast, and that thine hand might be with me, and that thou wouldest keep me from evil, that it may not grieve me! And God granted him that which he requested" (1 Chronicles 4:9-10).

In June 2010, when about 40 US Billionaires signed to give away majority of their wealth, they had their intentions stated clearly. In a letter explaining the reasons for his pledge, Mr. Weill and his wife, Joan, wrote that *"shrouds don't have pockets."* George Lucas, the creators of star wars, said he was dedicating his fortune to improving education. A few years ago, Mr. Buffett also pledged to give away 99 percent of his wealth.

> "⁴Now when he had left speaking, he said unto Simon, Launch out into the deep, and let down your nets for a draught. ⁵And Simon answering said unto him, Master, we have toiled all the night, and have taken nothing: nevertheless at thy word I will let down the net. ⁶And when they had this done, they inclosed a great multitude of fishes: and their net brake. ⁷And they beckoned unto their partners, which were in the

> *other ship, that they should come and help them. And they came, and filled both the ships, so that they began to sink. ⁸When Simon Peter saw it, he fell down at Jesus' knees, saying, Depart from me; for I am a sinful man, O Lord. ⁹For he was astonished, and all that were with him, at the draught of the fishes, which they had taken: ¹⁰And so was also James, and John, the sons of Zebedee, which were partners with Simon. And Jesus said unto Simon, Fear not; from henceforth thou shalt catch men"* (<u>Luke 5:4-10</u>).

God is more than ready to bless us always, and answer all our prayers than we are ready to pray. He is waiting for sincere believers to pray according to His will. <u>God wants to bless people, who will use His blessings to better the lives of others and promote His kingdom.</u> That's why He revealed that He gives wealth to establish His covenant.

> *"But thou shalt remember the* L<small>ORD</small> *thy God: for it is he that giveth thee power to get wealth, that he may establish his covenant which he sware unto thy fathers, as it is this day"* (<u>Deuteronomy 8:18</u>).

Therefore, if you are prepared to experience financial miracles, pray these prayers fervently and you will be favored exceedingly with financial miracles.

PRAYER POINTS

1. O Lord, arise and give me financial miracles today, in the name of Jesus.

2. Every enemy of my finance, be frustrated by fire, in the name of Jesus.

3. Every demonic hindrance to my financial miracles, disappear, in Jesus name.

4. I withdraw all my finances from satanic banks, in the name of Jesus.

5. O Lord, open a fresh account for me in heaven, in Jesus name.

6. Any strongman sitting upon my finances, collapse and die, in the name of Jesus.

7. Any evil personality sitting upon my possessions, I depose you by force, in the name of Jesus.

8. Any power that is stealing my money, be arrested and destroyed, in the name of Jesus.

9. Any satanic money in my possession, I reject you, in the name of Jesus.

10. My finances in the hand of the wicked, be released now, in the name of Jesus.

11. O Lord, send people that will bless me with finances, in the name of Jesus.

12. I gather my finances together to the glory of God, in the name of Jesus.

13. Blood of Jesus, speak my finances out of evil prisons, in the name of Jesus.

14. Any satanic agent with my finance, return them by force, in the name of Jesus.

15. Any evil hand stealing my money, wither by force, in the name of Jesus.

16. Let the financial miracle that will advertise me appear, in the name of Jesus.

17. O Lord, multiply my finances exceedingly, in the name of Jesus.

18. Let the business that will make me financially stronger worldwide appear by force, in the name of Jesus.

PRAYER FOR DIVINE BREAKTHROUGH

Breakthrough in every area of life is the promise of God to His people. This is believers' true inheritance. When you determine in your heart to do everything right to the glory of God, you will experience divine breakthrough in every area of your life.

> "⁹And Jabez was more honorable than his brethren: and his mother called his name Jabez, saying, Because I bare him with sorrow. ¹⁰And Jabez called on the God of Israel, saying, Oh that thou wouldest bless me indeed, and enlarge my coast, and that thine hand might be with me, and that thou wouldest keep me from evil, that it may not grieve me! And God granted him that which he requested" (1 Chronicles 4:9-10).

The question is, are you willing to use God's blessings to His glory; to propagate the gospel and help the less privileged? Two US billionaires, Bill Gates, the founder of Microsoft and Warren Buffett are putting the bulk of their fortunes into the Bill and Melinda Gates foundation, which fights diseases in the developing world and promotes education in the US. They have been searching for supporters for what they call *"The Giving Pledge"* after becoming concerned that the recession has cut into charity. What will you use your financial breakthrough for?

PRAYER POINTS

1. Every enemy of my breakthrough, be disgrace, in the name of Jesus.

2. I command my angel of breakthrough to manifest by force, in the name of Jesus.

3. Blood of Jesus, cover and protect my divine breakthrough, in the name of Jesus.

4. Anointing that disgraces enemies of breakthrough, possess me, in the name of Jesus.

5. Any area of my life under the oppression of poverty, receive deliverance, in the name of Jesus.

6. O Lord, arise and empower me for breakthrough, in the name of Jesus.

7. I cast out demons hindering my breakthrough, in the name of Jesus.

8. Father Lord, release my destiny from the grip of debts, in the name of Jesus.

9. Any strongman sitting upon my breakthrough, be unseated by death, in the name of Jesus.

10. Holy Ghost fire, burn marks of failure in my life, in the name of Jesus.

11. Lord Jesus, take me to the mountain of great success, in the name of Jesus.

12. O Lord, give me a business that will lead me into Your breakthrough, in the name of Jesus.

13. Any Goliath that is speaking against my breakthrough, die, in the name of Jesus.

14. Any evil personality that is standing against my breakthrough, be frustrated, in the name of Jesus.

15. Every yoke of hardship in my life, break to pieces, in the name of Jesus. *Matt 11*

16. Every inherited poverty and affliction in my life, be wasted, in the name of Jesus.

17. Every bondage of suffering in my life, break, in the name of Jesus.

18. Let the breakthrough that will advertise my greatness begin to manifest, in the name of Jesus.

19. Every dream of prosperity in my life, manifest by force, in the name of Jesus.

20. O Lord, arise and push my life forward, in the name of Jesus.

21. Any evil wall standing against my prosperity, collapse, in the name of Jesus.

22. O Lord, prosper me and take me to my promised land, in the name of Jesus.

23. By the anointing that God used to prosper Jabez, I prosper by force, in the name of Jesus.

PRAYER FOR DIVINE OPPORTUNITIES

Divine opportunities do not come by all the time. It is a good thing to ask God to help you recognize divine opportunities. However, you have to determine to overcome distractions, pleasures of sin and evil demands. Recall that Adam and Eve lost their blessings and divine opportunities when they ate the forbidden fruit. Cain lost his blessings and divine opportunity when he killed his brother, Abel.

> "*8And Cain talked with Abel his brother: and it came to pass, when they were in the field, that Cain rose up against Abel his brother, and slew him. 9And the LORD said unto Cain, Where is Abel thy brother? And he said, I know not: Am I my brother's keeper?"* (Genesis 4:8-9).

Lot lost his spiritual fortune, even before he entered Sodom, the very day he walked by sight.

> "*10And Lot lifted up his eyes, and beheld all the plain of Jordan, that it was well watered every where, before the LORD destroyed Sodom and Gomorrah, even as the garden of the LORD, like the land of Egypt, as thou comest unto Zoar. 11Then Lot chose him all the plain of Jordan; and Lot journeyed east: and they separated themselves the one from the other. 12Abram dwelled in the land of Canaan, and Lot dwelled in the cities of the plain, and pitched his tent toward Sodom. 13But the men of Sodom were wicked and sinners before the LORD exceedingly"* (Genesis 13:10-13).

Sarah, the wife of Abraham, brought sorrow to herself and unborn Isaac the day she handed her matrimonial home to her Egyptian maid, Hagar. Esau lost his blessings and divine opportunity when he sold his birthright to Jacob. Reuben lost his inheritance the day he slept with his father's concubine. The ten spies lost their lives and portions in the Promised Land when they delivered an evil report.

But Joseph's blessing, divine opportunity and answers to his prayers came after his faithfulness to God and decision not to sleep with his master's wife, and stand for righteousness at all cost. Enoch went to heaven for walking daily with God.

> "^{2}And the LORD was with Joseph, and he was a prosperous man; and he was in the house of his master the Egyptian… ^{6}And he left all that he had in Joseph's hand; and he knew not ought he had, save the bread which he did eat. And Joseph was a goodly person, and well favored… ^{10}And it came to pass, as she spake to Joseph day by day, that he hearkened not unto her, to lie by her, or to be with her. ^{11}And it came to pass about this time, that Joseph went into the house to do his business; and there was none of the men of the house there within" (Genesis 39:2, 6, 10-11).

> "^{23}And all the days of Enoch were three hundred sixty and five years: ^{24}And Enoch walked with God: and he was not; for God took him" (Genesis 5:23-24).

Determine in your heart to live right and be in right standing with God, and God is able to answer all your prayers and supply all that you need.

Tues July 21

PRAYER POINTS

1. I receive power to say no to sin, in the name of Jesus.

2. Any sin devil wants to accuse me of before God, I overcome you, in the name of Jesus.

3. Any evil plan to move me away from God, I terminate you by force, in the name of Jesus.

4. Any messenger of devil assigned to keeping me away from God, die, in the name of Jesus.

5. Holy Ghost fire, burn every enemy of my blessings, in the name of Jesus.

6. Any agent of devil that wants to keep me in sin, I resist you, in the name of Jesus.

7. Any demonic program designed to rob me of my greatness; I reject you, in the name of Jesus.

8. I receive power to say no to sin, in the name of Jesus.

9. O Lord, empower me to live right, even in the midst of trials and temptation, in the name of Jesus.

10. Blood of Jesus, wash me in and out, in the name of Jesus.

11. Father Lord, help me to walk into my blessings with less difficulty, in the name of Jesus.

12. Any evil program designed to divert me from divine plans, die, in the name of Jesus.

13. O Lord, take me to a place of divine opportunities, in the name of Jesus.

14. I receive the opportunity to appear before my helpers, in the name of Jesus.

15. Father Lord, help me to use every opportunity to please You, in the name of Jesus.
16. I receive the grace to fight my battles at the right time, in the name of Jesus.
17. Lord Jesus, empower me to confront my Goliath and conquer him, in the name of Jesus.
18. I receive boldness to step into places at the right times, in the name of Jesus.
19. Opportunity to become an international success, appear and bless me, in the name of Jesus.
20. I grab every opportunity that will make me great worldwide, in the name of Jesus.
21. I receive opportunity for all manner of breakthroughs forever, in the name of Jesus.

PRAYER FOR DIVINE CONNECTIONS

The best way to establish any connection is to connect to God first. Then through God's connection, connecting with men becomes meaningful and purposeful. Without connecting to God first, no human can rightly connect to any profitable relationship. We all need to be connected because no human can succeed alone on earth.

> *"^{18}And the LORD God said, It is not good that the man should be alone; I will make him an help meet for him"* (Genesis 2:18).

> *"^{9}Two are better than one; because they have a good reward for their labor. ^{10}For if they fall, the one will lift up his fellow: but woe to him that is alone when he falleth; for he hath not another to help him up. ^{11}Again, if two lie together, then they have heat: but how can one be warm alone? ^{12}And if one prevails against him, two shall withstand him; and a threefold cord is not quickly broken"* (Ecclesiastes 4:9-12).

God said that it is not good for a man to be alone. Also, we know that two are better than one. Apart from marriage relationship, every human needs to relate with other humans in all aspects of life. While in the natural body, God sets members as it pleases Him.

> *"^{11}But all these worketh that one and the selfsame Spirit, dividing to every man severally as he will... ^{18}But now hath God set the members every one of them in the body, as it hath pleased him. ^{28}And God hath set some in the church, first apostles, secondarily prophets, thirdly teachers, after that miracles, then gifts of healings, helps, governments, diversities of tongues"* (1 Corinthians 12:11, 18, 28).

We must prayerfully allow God to make choices for us. For God to guide our desires and aspirations, they must be in line with His plans and purpose. Pray that God connects you to right people, who are prepared to help you in life, in order to fully accomplish all that God purposes for you.

> "²As they ministered to the Lord, and fasted, the Holy Ghost said, Separate me Barnabas and Saul for the work whereunto I have called them. ³And when they had fasted and prayed, and laid their hands on them, they sent them away. ⁴So they, being sent forth by the Holy Ghost, departed unto Seleucia; and from thence they sailed to Cyprus" (Acts 13:2-4).

When you don't pray for divine connections, you are likely to keep meeting people, who will continue to hinder you from knowing or doing God's will. It is good to be born again. But when you ignore to pray for right connections, you may not fulfill your destiny on earth.

> "¹In the year that king Uzziah died I saw also the Lord sitting upon a throne, high and lifted up, and his train filled the temple. ²Above it stood the seraphims: each one had six wings; with twain he covered his face, and with twain he covered his feet, and with twain he did fly. ³And one cried unto another, and said, Holy, holy, holy, is the LORD of hosts: the whole earth is full of his glory. ⁴And the posts of the door moved at the voice of him that cried, and the house was filled with smoke. ⁵Then said I, Woe is me! for I am undone; because I am a man of unclean lips, and I dwell in the midst of a people of unclean lips: for mine eyes have seen the King, the LORD of hosts. ⁶Then flew one of the seraphims unto me, having a live coal in his hand, which he had taken with the tongs from off the altar: ⁷And he laid it upon my mouth, and said, Lo, this hath touched thy lips; and thine iniquity is taken away, and thy sin purged. ⁸Also I heard the voice of the Lord, saying, Whom shall I send, and who will go for us? Then said I, Here am I; send me" (Isaiah 6:1-8).

When you keep connecting with wrong people, you may never experience divine visitation that can turn your life around for good. You will remain spiritually blinded and unable to know how holy, powerful and glorious God is. You will remain seeing the glory of men; serving men instead of serving God. Praying for divine connection helps you to discover yourself first, your destiny and tapping directly from resources of heaven.

Though sometimes you may be deceived to believe you have arrived without praying for any divine connection. But it doesn't always happen that way. What is important is that you connect with God first. Then when you connect to God, He is able to link you up with the right helpers and supporters, who will be competing to do you good instead of evil. Even when severe battles confront with, you still see helpers come to your rescue.

Be mindful also that if sin is still reigning in your life, it will prevent you from hearing and answering God's call.

> "¹David therefore departed thence, and escaped to the cave Adullam: and when his brethren and all his father's house heard it, they went down thither to him. ²And every one that was in distress, and every one that was in debt, and every one that was discontented, gathered themselves unto him; and he became a captain over them: and there were with him about four hundred men" (1 Samuel 22:1-2).

> "⁵Peter therefore was kept in prison: but prayer was made without ceasing of the church unto God for him. ⁶And when Herod would have brought him forth, the same night Peter was sleeping between two soldiers, bound with two chains: and the keepers before the door kept the prison. ⁷And, behold, the angel of the Lord came upon him, and a light shined in the prison: and he smote Peter on the side, and raised him up, saying, Arise up quickly. And his chains fell off from his hands" (Acts 12:5-7).

When God establishes you, helpers will locate you, assist you and be ready to die for you, if need be.

> "²And David sent forth a third part of the people under the hand of Joab, and a third part under the hand of Abishai the son of Zeruiah, Joab's brother, and a third part under the hand of Ittai the Gittite. And the king said unto the people, I will surely go forth with you myself also. ³But the people answered, Thou shalt not go forth: for if we flee away, they will not care for us; neither if half of us die, will they care for us: but now thou art worth ten thousand of us: therefore now it is better that thou succour us out of the city" (2 Samuel 18:2-3).

> "¹⁴And David was then in an hold, and the garrison of the "Philistines was then in Beth–lehem. ¹⁵And David longed, and said, Oh that one would give me drink of the water of the well of Beth–lehem, which is by the gate! ¹⁶And the three mighty men brake through the host of the Philistines, and drew water out of the well of Beth–lehem, that was by the gate, and took it, and brought it to David: nevertheless he would not drink thereof, but poured it out unto the LORD. ¹⁷And he said, Be it far from me, O LORD, that I should do this: is not this the blood of the men that went in jeopardy of their lives? Therefore he would not drink it. These things did these three mighty men" (2 Samuel 23:14-17).

I suppose that more than half of the earth's populations are involved in wrong relationships, connections and other things. Millions of people are into wrong marriages. Others are living in wrong places and doing wrong jobs. But with the help of the Almighty, the prayers in this book will guide you to pray for right and divine connections. Someone, who approaches God, must approach Him with praises and thanksgiving, a fervent prayer and truthful heart. It is well with you in Jesus name, Amen.

Wed 7/22/15
@ Golden Coral
Asheboro

PRAYER POINTS

1. Father Lord, arise and mark me for divine connections, in the name of Jesus.

2. Blood of Jesus, connect me with my true helpers in life, in the name of Jesus.

3. Holy Ghost fire, burn any evil mark in my life, in the name of Jesus.

4. Let the power of God link me up with heavenly angels, in the name of Jesus.

5. I receive power to connect with people that matters, in the name of Jesus.

6. Any evil inscription in my life, spiritual or physical, catch fire, in the name of Jesus.

7. Let my life be empowered to attract unmerited favors, in the name of Jesus.

8. O Lord, connect me with people that will favor me exceedingly, in the name of Jesus.

9. Any curse in my life that is separating me from people in authority, expire, in the name of Jesus.

10. I command every satanic mark or stamp in my body to disappear, in the name of Jesus.

11. Blood of Jesus, beautify me to be acceptable everywhere I go, in the name of Jesus.

12. Angels of the living God, take me to right places at right times, in the name of Jesus.

13. O Lord, arise and ordain me for honor and blessing, in the name of Jesus.

14. I receive anointing for great people to seek my services, in the name of Jesus.

15. Father Lord, connect me to all manner of blessings forever, in the name of Jesus.

16. Every weapon of rejection prepared against me, catch fire, in the name of Jesus.

17. I bind evil eyes assigned to monitor my blessings, in the name of Jesus.

18. Lord Jesus, connect me to people that are determined to help me succeed, in the name of Jesus.

19. I receive the grace of God to connect to the good things of life, in the name of Jesus.

PRAYER FOR BUSINESS BREAKTHROUGH

People, who use their wealth and breakthrough to reconcile many other people to God, will experience more and more breakthrough. These people are actively engaged in God's ministry of reconciliation.

> "*[18] And all things are of God, who hath reconciled us to himself by Jesus Christ, and hath given to us the ministry of reconciliation*" (2 Corinthians 5:18).

Also notice that no one can steal from God and becomes innocent or qualified for more blessing.

> "*[8] Will a man rob God? Yet ye have robbed me. But ye say, Wherein have we robbed thee? In tithes and offerings. [9] Ye are cursed with a curse: for ye have robbed me, even this whole nation. [10] Bring ye all the tithes into the storehouse, that there may be meat in mine house, and prove me now herewith, saith the LORD of hosts, if I will not open you the windows of heaven, and pour you out a blessing, that there shall not be room enough to receive it. [11] And I will rebuke the devourer for your sakes, and he shall not destroy the fruits of your ground; neither shall your vine cast her fruit before the time in the field, saith the LORD of hosts. [12] And all nations shall call you blessed: for ye shall be a delightsome land, saith the LORD of hosts*" (Malachi 3:8-12).

> "*[38] Give, and it shall be given unto you; good measure, pressed down, and shaken together, and running over, shall men give into your bosom. For with the same measure that ye mete withal it shall be measured to you again*" (Luke 6:38).

The determination of the American billionaires to give more than 50 percent of their entire wealth is a challenge to other rich people in the world. They are symbolic of a rebuke to all selfish people in the world, especially Africa, in general, and Nigeria, in particular. If you have determined to be a giver, the prayers in this section will bless you the more.

Thurs 7/23/15

PRAYER POINTS

1. I command every good door for business breakthrough to open for me, in the name of Jesus.

2. Any power that is blocking my breakthroughs, be paralyzed by force, in the name of Jesus.

3. Every satanic stronghold blocking my vision for business breakthrough, collapse, in the name of Jesus.

4. I bind and cast out every strongman hindering my business, in the name of Jesus.

5. Every spirit of hell and destruction attacking my business, be frustrated, in the name of Jesus.

6. Any power that is sponsoring business failures, I am not your candidate, be arrested to death, in the name of Jesus.

7. Any curse placed upon my business, expire by force, in the name of Jesus.

8. Every spirit of disappointment upon my business, be cast out, in the name of Jesus.

9. Any evil power manipulating my business, be frustrated, in the name of Jesus.

10. O Lord, arise and prosper my business by fire, in the name of Jesus.

11. Any evil padlock over my business, break to pieces, in the name of Jesus.

12. Every agent of the devourer against my business, die, in the name of Jesus.

13. Every satanic yoke upon my business, break to pieces, in the name of Jesus.

14. Blood of Jesus, speak divine breakthrough unto my business, in the name of Jesus.

15. I receive power for supernatural breakthrough in my business, in the name of Jesus.

16. Any demonic limitation placed upon my business, disappear, in the name of Jesus.

17. Holy Ghost power, break every bondage against my business, in the name of Jesus.

18. Every hedge of thorns built around my business, catch fire, in the name of Jesus.

19. O Lord, give me a business breakthrough that will advertise me to the world, in the name of Jesus.

PRAYER FOR DIVINE PROMOTION

Seeking for promotion outside God and His Word is elusive and of no use. People, who search for promotions through many other means, do not receive true promotion. That's why many people have paid costly prices, even with their lives. You cannot receive any free and true gift from Satan. You must pay a price at initial or later stage.

> "⁶For promotion cometh neither from the east, nor from the west, nor from the south. ⁷But God is the judge: he putteth down one, and setteth up another. ⁸For in the hand of the LORD there is a cup, and the wine is red; it is full of mixture; and he poureth out of the same: but the dregs thereof, all the wicked of the earth shall wring them out, and drink them" (Psalms 75:6-8).

Determine to trust God for promotion and blessing, no matter how long it lasts. But if you are not born-again yet, you must be born-again before God can promote and bless you. More so, you need to be aware that Satan do promote people also, and easily. Even his agents and demons can do the same. But like I mentioned earlier, you must pay a price for their promotions, and your sorrows will increase.

> "²⁸Hast thou not known? Hast thou not heard that the everlasting God, the LORD, the Creator of the ends of the earth, fainteth not, neither is weary? There is no searching of his understanding. ²⁹He giveth power to the faint; and to them that have no might he increaseth strength. ³⁰Even the youths shall faint and be weary, and the young men shall utterly fall: ³¹But they that wait upon the LORD shall renew their strength; they shall mount up with wings as eagles; they shall run, and not be weary; and they shall walk, and not faint" (Isaiah 40: 28-31).

It is better and safer to please God, and then pray and wait for His blessings and promotion. In fact, avoid the devil at all cost. When God's promotion comes, every other need becomes insignificant.

> *"⁷When a man's ways please the LORD, he maketh even his enemies to be at peace with him"* (Proverbs 16:7).

In my lifetime, I have seen only a few people enjoying God's true blessings. You become one of such people, if you believe it in your heart, as you pray and trust God in this program.

PRAYER POINTS

1. O Lord, arise in Your power and promote me forever, in the name of Jesus.

2. Blood of Jesus, speak promotion into my life by fire, in the name of Jesus.

3. Every enemy of my promotion, die, in the name of Jesus.

4. Any seed of demotion planted against me, die by force, in the name of Jesus.

5. I withdraw my destiny from the captivity of failures, in the name of Jesus.

6. O Lord, promote me to the next level, in the name of Jesus.

7. Any power blocking my promotion, be frustrated, in the name of Jesus.

8. Any witch or wizard standing against my promotion, fail, in the name of Jesus.

9. Heavenly father, initiate my promotion from heaven, in the name of Jesus.

10. Holy Ghost fire, burn every enemy of my promotion, in the name of Jesus.

11. Let every satanic mark chasing away my promotion, die, in the name of Jesus.

12. Any evil womb that has swallowed my promotion, open and vomit it by force, in the name of Jesus.

13. O Lord, promote me to unimaginable heights, in the name of Jesus.

14. Let my enemies proclaim my promotion forever, in the name of Jesus.

15. Every agent of darkness that has stolen my promotion, release it, in the name of Jesus.

16. Any grave that has buried my promotion, open and release it, in the name of Jesus.

17. Any witchcraft power holding my promotion, die, in the name of Jesus.

18. Let the wind of destruction destroy every enemy of my promotion, in the name of Jesus.

19. O Lord, arise and promote me by fire, in the name of Jesus.

PRAYER FOR PROSPERITY

Prosperity is a condition of enjoying wealth, success and good fortune. Therefore, to prosper and enjoy godly prosperity, your life has to be surrender to God first as you seek the kingdom of God and His righteousness. You have to accept and respect the fact that God owns the entire universe. God owns your life, time and all possession. Understanding this truth will help you submit everything to Him. No one enjoys godly prosperity except he allows God to control the wealth.

> "³But know that the LORD hath set apart him that is godly for himself: the LORD will hear when I call unto him" (Psalms 4:3).

> "¹⁴Behold, the heaven and the heaven of heavens is the LORD'S thy God, the earth also, with all that therein is"(Deuteronomy 10:14).

> "⁸The silver is mine, and the gold is mine, saith the LORD of hosts" (Haggai 2:8).

The earth and its fullness thereof belong to the Almighty God. Even believers belong to Him by the means of creation and by redemption.

> "³³But seek ye first the kingdom of God, and his righteousness; and all these things shall be added unto you" (Matthew 6:33).

> "⁹But ye are a chosen generation, a royal priesthood, an holy nation, a peculiar people; that ye should shew forth the praises of him who hath called you out of darkness into his marvelous light" (1 Peter 2:9).

It is useless to possess massive wealth without reference to God. Learn to trust God and surrender your time, money and talents to Him.

Sat July 25, 2015

PRAYER POINTS

1. O Lord, let my prosperity originate from You, in the name of Jesus.

2. Any evil power against my prosperity, be arrested, in the name of Jesus.

3. Father Lord, give me godly prosperity that will swallow my poverty, in the name of Jesus.

4. Holy Ghost power, fall upon me and prosper me greatly, in the name of Jesus.

5. Any covenant of poverty in my life, break, in the name of Jesus.

6. Any curse of poverty in my life, expire, in the name of Jesus.

7. Any bewitchment against my prosperity, be lifted, in the name of Jesus.

8. Any evil sacrifice against my prosperity, expire, in the name of Jesus.

9. Blood of Jesus, speak prosperity into my life, in the name of Jesus.

10. Every enemy of my prosperity, be exposed and disgraced, in the name of Jesus.

11. Any power that has vowed to keep me in poverty, die, in the name of Jesus.

12. O Lord, arise and enlarge my coast greatly, in the name of Jesus.

13. O Lord, give me a contract that will announce my life to the world, in the name of Jesus.

14. Let the strongman against my prosperity die, in the name of Jesus.

15. I receive the wisdom and God's knowledge to prosper, in the name of Jesus.

16. Let the angels of God escort me into the camp of prosperity, in the name of Jesus.

17. O Lord, clothe me with the garment of prosperity, in the name of Jesus.

18. I receive all manner of prosperity by only the power of God, in the name of Jesus.

PRAYER FOR PROTECTION FROM ENEMIES

Satan and all his demons are mankind's greatest enemies. Their chief weapon is sin. That's why when you break the hedge of protection of God through sin, the serpent (Satan) bites you (*See* Ecclesiastes 10:8). But when God is protecting or shielding His people from enemies of their souls, the saints can easily overcome every other worldly problem and challenges without much struggle.

> "*[10]The thief cometh not, but for to steal, and to kill, and to destroy: I am come that they might have life, and that they might have it more abundantly*" (John 10:10).

> "*[14]Afterward Jesus findeth him in the temple, and said unto him, Behold, thou art made whole: sin no more, lest a worse thing come unto thee*" (John 5:14).

Before praying for protection and deliverance from household enemies, witches and wizards, repent truthfully from your sins and confess them to God. Otherwise, you may bring more harm upon yourself by praying against demonic people. Demons have the power to deal with you severely through any trace of sin in your life. Perpetual or prevailing sins in peoples' lives often fuel most problems and difficulties affecting them. Even Satan cannot function effectively in places where there is no sin or disobedience to God's law.

> "*[14]If my people, which are called by my name, shall humble themselves, and pray, and seek my face, and turn from their wicked ways; then will I hear from heaven, and will forgive their sin, and will heal their land*" (2 Chronicles 7:14).

The backbone of our greatest enemy, which is Satan, can be broken easily when the issue of sin is settled. Prayer for protection from enemies receives answers as soon as people deal with sin.

Sun July 26

PRAYERS POINTS

1. O Lord, create an iron wall to protect me from my enemies' wrath, in the name of Jesus.

2. Divine whirlwind, carry the weapons of my enemies back to them, in the name of Jesus.

3. I command my enemies to get enough confusion by force, in the name of Jesus.

4. Any determined enemy against my life, receive shock, in the name of Jesus.

5. Let the wisdom of my enemies convert to foolishness, in the name of Jesus.

6. Let my enemies mistakenly use weapons they prepared for me on themselves, in the name of Jesus.

7. O Lord, block my enemies from harming me by any means, in the name of Jesus.

8. Father Lord, withdraw the helpers of my enemies, in the name of Jesus.

9. Let the handwriting of my enemies turn against them, in the name of Jesus.

10. Blood of Jesus, protect me from enemy attacks, in the name of Jesus.

11. Holy Ghost fire, burn every determined enemy of my destiny, in the name of Jesus.

12. Let the rage of my enemies turn against them, in the name of Jesus.

13. Angels of the living God, stop my enemies from their wickedness, in the name of Jesus.

14. I command my enemies to fall into the pit they dug against me, in the name of Jesus.

15. Let the fire of God burn my enemies' plans, in the name of Jesus.

16. I command my enemies to make a mistake that will favor me, in the name of Jesus.

17. Let the brain of my enemies scatter and destroy their evil plans, in the name of Jesus.

18. Let all creatures arise as instrument of protection for my sake, in the name of Jesus.

PRAYER FOR PROTECTION FROM EVIL

The earth is filled with plentiful evil operations. That's why we all need protection from evil. The Scriptures revealed that Satan, the thief, comes to steal, kill and destroy. But none of these will be your portion in Jesus name.

> "[15]The eyes of the LORD are upon the righteous, and his ears are open unto their cry. [16]The face of the LORD is against them that do evil, to cut off the remembrance of them from the earth. [17]The righteous cry, and the LORD heareth, and delivereth them out of all their troubles. [18]The LORD is nigh unto them that are of a broken heart; and saveth such as be of a contrite spirit. [19]Many are the afflictions of the righteous: but the LORD delivereth him out of them all. [20]He keepeth all his bones: not one of them is broken. [21]Evil shall slay the wicked: and they that hate the righteous shall be desolate. [22]The LORD redeemeth the soul of his servants: and none of them that trust in him shall be desolate" (Psalms 34:15-22).

Through our prayers of faith and trust in God, He watches over us. His presence and power sustain, heal, support and protect us from the attacks of the wicked one.

> "[6]The LORD is on my side; I will not fear: what can man do unto me? [7]The LORD taketh my part with them that help me: therefore shall I see my desire upon them that hate me. [8]It is better to trust in the LORD than to put confidence in man. [9]It is better to trust in the LORD than to put confidence in princes" (Psalms 118:6-9).

In distress or trouble, pray for God's protection. God responds to our prayers when are in trouble. He will not abandon you in time of distress.

"⁸Depart from me, all ye workers of iniquity; for the LORD hath heard the voice of my weeping" (Psalms 6:8).

> *"⁸And when he had taken the book, the four beasts and four and twenty elders fell down before the Lamb, having every one of them harps, and golden vials full of odors, which are the prayers of saints"* (Revelation 5:8).

Jesus Christ is the rock of our salvation, refuge and deliverance, especially in times of trouble. Trusting and having confidence in Him is our only place of safety. He is always there to take your burden and give you rest. Therefore, when problems and enemies increase, make it known to God in prayers. He is able to rise and fight for you. You need to pray for divine protection.

PRAYER POINTS

1. Any power that is exposing me to satanic attacks, receive blindness, in the name of Jesus.

2. Every arrow of sin fired into my life, I fire you back, in the name of Jesus.

3. Blood of Jesus, flow into my life and protect me from destruction, in the name of Jesus.

4. Let soldiers of Christ arise and protect me from all evil, in the name of Jesus.

5. Every negative action taken to destroy me, fail woefully, in the name of Jesus.

6. Any evil arrow fired to waste my life, go back to your sender, in the name of Jesus.

7. O Lord, protect me from destiny destroyers, in the name of Jesus.

8. Father Lord, make my life invisible from destiny killers, in the name of Jesus.

9. Wherever my enemies are waiting for me, O Lord, protect me, in the name of Jesus.

10. Let the angels of God protect me from satanic demons, in the name of Jesus.

11. I command my life to be preserved from evil attacks, in the name of Jesus.

12. Father Lord, protect me from my evil family pattern, in the name of Jesus.

13. Any evil power assigned to waste me, fail woefully, in the name of Jesus.

14. O Lord, deliver me from failures, in the name of Jesus.

15. I receive divine protection from accident and death, in the name of Jesus.

16. Lord Jesus, protect me from evil inversions, in the name of Jesus.

17. I receive protection from all manner of sickness and diseases, in the name of Jesus.

18. I receive protection from local and international disasters, in the name of Jesus.

19. My Father, deliver me from journey to hell fire, in the name of Jesus.

PRAYER FOR DELIVERANCE FROM POVERTY

A state of not having money to take care of basic needs such as food, clothing, and housing is indeed a very cruel state. The spirit of poverty is a very wicked spirit and tyrant that can exercise absolute control over the life of a person, family, place or nation. You need deliverance from this spirit. If you don't destroy poverty as soon as possible, by the grace of the Almighty God, poverty destroys you. When Jabez discovered the spirit poverty in his foundation, he began praying for deliverance.

> "⁹And Jabez was more honorable than his brethren: and his mother called his name Jabez, saying, Because I bare him with sorrow. ¹⁰And Jabez called on the God of Israel, saying, Oh that thou wouldest bless me indeed, and enlarge my coast, and that thine hand might be with me, and that thou wouldest keep me from evil, that it may not grieve me! And God granted him that which he requested" (1 Chronicles 4:9-10).

I believe that this program will be very helpful to you as you call on the God of prosperity to deliver you from the spirit of poverty, and prosper you.

> "³Call unto me, and I will answer thee, and shew thee great and mighty things, which thou knowest not" (Jeremiah 33:3).

> "⁴For since the beginning of the world men have not heard, nor perceived by the ear, neither hath the eye seen, O God, beside thee, what he hath prepared for him that waiteth for him" (Isaiah 64:4).

There are blessings stored up for you in the heavenly warehouse, which your prayers can release. Poverty is not the will of God for your life. God made enough provisions for you ever before you were born. It's my prayer that as you pray these prayers, your life will experience a divine transformation, from poverty to prosperity.

PRAYER POINTS

1. I command poverty and debts in my life to bow out now, in the name of Jesus.

2. Let prosperity appear and swallow the spirit of poverty by fire, in the name of Jesus.

3. O Lord, release me from the bondage of poverty and debts, in the name of Jesus.

4. Every yoke of poverty and debts in my life, break, in the name of Jesus.

5. Father Lord, chase away poverty from my life forever, in the name of Jesus.

6. I command every arrow of poverty in my life to backfire, in the name of Jesus.

7. Blood of Jesus, flow into my foundation and destroy poverty spirit, in the name of Jesus.

8. Let the root of poverty in my life dry up and die, in the name of Jesus.

9. I recover double all that my ancestors handed over to devil, in the name of Jesus.

10. You, that fish that has swallowed my finances, vomit it now, in the name of Jesus.

11. Every enemy of my prosperity, die, in the name of Jesus.

12. Holy Ghost fire, burn every emblem of poverty in my life, in the name of Jesus.

13. I command the backbone of poverty and debts to break in my life, in the name of Jesus.

14. Any fire of poverty burning in my life, be quenched, in the name of Jesus.

15. Every garment of poverty in my life, catch fire, in the name of Jesus.

16. Lord Jesus, deliver me from poverty spirit, in the name of Jesus.

17. Any seed of poverty in my life, die, in the name of Jesus.

18. Let every shame that poverty has brought into my life disappear, in the name of Jesus.

19. O Lord, arise and make me greatly rich in this life, in the name of Jesus.

20. Any agent of oppression in my life, your time is up, die, in the name of Jesus.

21. I command poverty to receive double destruction, in the name of Jesus.

22. Any serpent of poverty on suicide mission in my life, die alone, in the name of Jesus.

PRAYER TO OVERCOME ENEMIES IN THE PLACE OF WORK

Until God determines that you resign from you job and take up another job, you don't have any reason to resign your job in fear of enemies in your place of work. No one has ever solved any problem by running away from it. Learn to face your problems and trust God to help you overcome them. Even when the number of enemies in your place of work increases, you are not the person to go. They are to go for your sake instead.

> "^{4}Then the presidents and princes sought to find occasion against Daniel concerning the kingdom; but they could find none occasion nor fault; forasmuch as he was faithful, neither was there any error or fault found in him. ^{5}Then said these men, We shall not find any occasion against this Daniel, except we find it against him concerning the law of his God... ^{16}Then the king commanded, and they brought Daniel, and cast him into the den of lions. Now the king spake and said unto Daniel, Thy God whom thou servest continually, he will deliver thee... ^{18}Then the king went to his palace, and passed the night fasting: neither were instruments of musick brought before him: and his sleep went from him" (Daniel 6:4-5, 16, 18).

When God gives you a job, you don't have any reason to abandon it out of fear. God, who started every good thing in your life, is able to bring all to completion. Trust Him.

> "^{23}Then was the king exceeding glad for him, and commanded that they should take Daniel up out of the den. So Daniel was taken up out of the den, and no manner of hurt was found upon him, because he believed in his God. ^{24}And the king commanded, and

they brought those men which had accused Daniel, and they cast them into the den of lions, them, their children, and their wives; and the lions had the mastery of them, and brake all their bones in pieces or ever they came at the bottom of the den" (Daniel 6:23-24).

As you do your job diligently, without any compromise with devil and his agents, you will overcome all your problems in Jesus name, Amen.

PRAYER POINTS

1. O Lord, deliver me from problems in my place of work, in the name of Jesus.

2. Any trap set for me in my place of work, catch your owner, in the name of Jesus.

3. O Lord, help me to avoid deadly mistakes in the office, in the name of Jesus.

4. Let satanic attacks against me in my place of work end, in the name of Jesus.

5. Let my enemies in the office be transferred, in the name of Jesus.

6. O Lord, replace my enemies in the office with people who will love me, in the name of Jesus.

7. Father, give me favor before people, who will decide my case, in the name of Jesus.

8. Let every decision-maker in office decide on my promotion, in the name of Jesus.

9. Any strongman assigned to trouble me in my office, be troubled, in the name of Jesus.

10. Let the choice of those, who oppose my promotion and progress in the office be overruled, in the name of Jesus.

11. Whosoever will go on transfer, resign or be dismissed for me to have rest, go, in the name of Jesus.

12. O Lord, arise and cause me to get the best in this office, in the name of Jesus.

13. Whoever has vowed to disgraced me out of this office, be disgraced, in the name of Jesus.

14. Any evil record designed to implicate me, be used for my advancement, in the name of Jesus.

15. O Lord, plan my way to the top in this office by force, in the name of Jesus.

16. I receive God's grace to excel above my contemporaries and bosses, in the name of Jesus.

17. O Lord, create more room for me to be catapulted to greatness everywhere I go, in the name of Jesus.

18. Any problem or weakness that is designed to demote me, die and die again, in the name of Jesus.

19. Every demonic opinion against me, be converted to favor, in the name of Jesus.

20. Let evil collaborators in this office be sacked, in the name of Jesus.

21. Let stubborn enemies write their letters of resignation by force immediately, in the name of Jesus

PRAYER TO PAY BILLS PROMPTLY

We are living in a time of distress and economic recession. Many people can no longer afford to train their children in schools, or pay their bills. This is a very negative trend, which have affected millions of people already.

> "*^{24}And it came to pass after this, that Ben–hadad king of Syria gathered all his host, and went up, and besieged Samaria. ^{25}And there was a great famine in Samaria: and, behold, they besieged it, until an ass's head was sold for fourscore pieces of silver, and the fourth part of a cab of dove's dung for five pieces of silver. ^{26}And as the king of Israel was passing by upon the wall, there cried a woman unto him, saying, Help, my lord, O king. ^{27}And he said, If the LORD do not help thee, whence shall I help thee? out of the barn floor, or out of the winepress? ^{28}And the king said unto her, What aileth thee? And she answered, This woman said unto me, Give thy son, that we may eat him to day, and we will eat my son to morrow. ^{29}So we boiled my son, and did eat him: and I said unto her on the next day, Give thy son, that we may eat him: and she hath hid her son*" (<u>2 Kings 6:24-29</u>).

We use terms like 'global roadblock' and 'economic meltdown' to describe current global predicament. Many people have taken to different directions. Everyone needs shelter, pay bills and meet up with responsibilities. Many can no longer meet up with these things. No jobs. There are regular salary cuts. Governments continue to define measures that have not helped.

> "*^{32}And ye shall know the truth, and the truth shall make you free… ^{36}If the Son therefore shall make you free, ye shall be free indeed*" (<u>John 8:32</u>).

> *"⁷And also I have withholden the rain from you, when there were yet three months to the harvest: and I caused it to rain upon one city, and caused it not to rain upon another city: one piece was rained upon, and the piece whereupon it rained not withered"* (Amos 4:7).

Yet in all these troubles, the world has failed to recognize that God is the only way out, as revealed through His only begotten Son, Jesus Christ. But to them who repent and surrender their lives to Christ, He shows the way out of all troubles. I pray that God favors your business, job, life and family so you could pay all your bills in the name of Jesus.

PRAYER POINTS

1. O Lord, arise and help me to pay my bills promptly, in the name of Jesus.

2. Any problem that has rendered me penniless, receive solution, in the name of Jesus.

3. Every arrow of financial problem fired at me, I fire you back, in the name of Jesus.

4. Let the backbone of poverty in my life be broken, in the name of Jesus.

5. Any evil personality sitting upon my prosperity, be unseated, in the name of Jesus.

6. Any power expanding my financial problems, die, in the name of Jesus.

7. O Lord, give me a breakthrough that will help me, in the name of Jesus.

8. I command every financial problem in my life to perish, in the name of Jesus.

9. Ancient of days, help me to pay my bills by Your power, in the name of Jesus.

10. I receive divine prosperity that will remain forever, in the name of Jesus.

11. Any inherited bondage in my life, break by force, in the name of Jesus.

12. I command any resident evil power attacking my finance to die, in the name of Jesus.

13. O Lord, deliver me from financial predicament, in the name of Jesus.

Today

14. I receive enough money to clear all my debts, in the name of Jesus.

15. Any outstanding bill in my life, be cleared now, in the name of Jesus.

16. Let every distributor of shame in my life die by force, in the name of Jesus.

17. O Lord, perfect Your help in my life, in the name of Jesus.

18. Any evil program going on against my life, be terminated, in the name of Jesus.

19. Father Lord, make a way for me where there is no way, in the name of Jesus.

From Prayer Retreat pg 148
Lord Show me a way out of all my Problem This year in The name of Jesus

PRAYER TO PROSPER IN BUSINESS

When you take care of God's business and His children, He takes care of yours and blesses it too. This is a principle many businessmen and women have failed to understand. The Scriptures revealed that the more you give, the more you receive. I pray that God blesses Bill Gates, Warren Buffett and 40 other American billionaires, who made a commitment, together with star wars' director, George Lucas, to provide an estimated $250 billion to help the less privileged people all over the world. I also pray that the recipients would not only benefit from the material aspect, but also spiritually see God as blessing and satisfying their needs.

> "*[16]For God so loved the world, that he gave his only begotten Son, that whosoever believeth in him should not perish, but have everlasting life. [17]For God sent not his Son into the world to condemn the world; but that the world through him might be saved. [18]He that believeth on him is not condemned: but he that believeth not is condemned already, because he hath not believed in the name of the only begotten Son of God. [19]And this is the condemnation, that light is come into the world, and men loved darkness rather than light, because their deeds were evil. [20]For every one that doeth evil hateth the light, neither cometh to the light, lest his deeds should be reproved. [21]But he that doeth truth cometh to the light, that his deeds may be made manifest, that they are wrought in God*" (John 3:16-21).

> "*[3]Jesus answered and said unto him, Verily, verily, I say unto thee, Except a man be born again, he can not see the kingdom of God*" (John 3:3).

If your heart is right with God, and your decision is to honor Him and better other peoples' lives, your prayers in this section will surely be answered.

> "⁶*But this I say, He which soweth sparingly shall reap also sparingly; and he which soweth bountifully shall reap also bountifully. ⁷Every man according as he purposeth in his heart, so let him give; not grudgingly, or of necessity: for God loveth a cheerful giver. ⁸And God is able to make all grace abound toward you; that ye, always having all sufficiency in all things, may abound to every good work: ⁹(As it is written, He hath dispersed abroad; he hath given to the poor: his righteousness remaineth for ever. ¹⁰Now he that ministereth seed to the sower both minister bread for your food, and multiply your seed sown, and increase the fruits of your righteousness;) ¹¹Being enriched in everything to all bountifulness, which causeth through us thanksgiving to God"* (2 Corinthians 9:6-11).

It is a sin to keep your wealth to yourself while billions of souls languish in sin and their bodies eaten up by hunger. I pray that God blesses your business so you can use it to the glory of His name and service to humanity.

PRAYER POINTS

1. Every enemy of my success in business, be disgraced, in the name of Jesus.

2. You, the heaven of my success, open by force, in the name of Jesus.

3. I command the favor of God to fall upon my business, in the name of Jesus.

4. Every arrow of failure fired at my business, backfire, in the name of Jesus.

5. Let the strongman of failures in my business, die, in the name of Jesus.

6. I dispatch the angels of business success into my business, in the name of Jesus.

7. I frustrate all satanic bad blood against my business, in the name of Jesus.

8. Let the blood of Jesus speak true success into my business, in the name of Jesus.

9. O Lord, arise and favor my business by force, in the name of Jesus.

10. O Lord, release the rain of abundance upon my business, in the name of Jesus.

11. Let the angels of miracles visit my business now, in the name of Jesus.

12. I receive open heaven for my business by force, in the name of Jesus.

13. Father Lord, create a channel of success into my business, in the name of Jesus.

14. I roll away every stone of hindrance against my business, in the name of Jesus.

15. Any strongman standing against my business, I command you to die, in the name Jesus.

16. Let the favor of God bring down divine success in my business, in the name of Jesus.

17. Any evil wind directed at my business, disappear, in the name of Jesus.

18. Every arrow of devil fired at my business, I fire you back, in the name of Jesus.

19. Blood of Jesus, speak life and prosperity into my business, in the name of Jesus.

the house, fell sick; and his sickness was so sore, that there was no breath left in him. ¹⁸And she said unto Elijah, What have I to do with thee, O thou man of God? art thou come unto me to call my sin to remembrance, and to slay my son? ¹⁹And he said unto her, Give me thy son. And he took him out of her bosom, and carried him up into a loft, where he abode, and laid him upon his own bed. ²⁰And he cried unto the LORD, and said, O LORD my God, hast thou also brought evil upon the widow with whom I sojourn, by slaying her son? ²¹And he stretched himself upon the child three times, and cried unto the LORD, and said, O LORD my God, I pray thee, let this child's soul come into him again. ²²And the LORD heard the voice of Elijah; and the soul of the child came into him again, and he revived" (1 Kings 17:16-22).

One, who is connected with God and His people, cannot be swallowed by any kind of trouble or problems. It is not possible.

"⁷When a man's ways please the LORD, he maketh even his enemies to be at peace with him" (Proverbs 16:7).

God knows how to connect you with people that really matters in the society. But without connecting with God first, no one can rightly connect to any profitable relationship that leads to eternity.

"¹⁸And the LORD God said, It is not good that the man should be alone; I will make him an help meet for him" (Genesis 2:18).

"⁹Two are better than one; because they have a good reward for their labor. ¹⁰For if they fall, the one will lift up his fellow: but woe to him that is alone when he falleth; for he hath not another to help him up. ¹¹Again, if two lie together, then they have heat: but how can one be warm alone? ¹²And if one prevail against him, two shall withstand him; and a threefold cord is not quickly broken" (Ecclesiastes 4:9-12).

PRAYER FOR DIVINE CONNECTIONS

A popular adage says that no man is an island. Truly, no one can survive in this by being alone. Therefore, a great business network is the backbone of all successful businesses. Without functional network, a business is good as dead. That's why businessmen and woman ought to pray for divine connections. However, the most important connection one can ever receive on earth is to be connected with God through the gift of salvation.

> "³Jesus answered and said unto him, Verily, verily, I say unto thee, Except a man be born again, he can not see the kingdom of God" (John 3:3).

> "⁸And it fell on a day, that Elisha passed to Shunem, where was a great woman; and she constrained him to eat bread. And so it was, that as oft as he passed by, he turned in thither to eat bread. ⁹And she said unto her husband, Behold now, I perceive that this is an holy man of God, which passeth by us continually... ¹⁶And he said, About this season, according to the time of life, thou shalt embrace a son. And she said, Nay, my lord, thou man of God, do not lie unto thine handmaid. ¹⁷And the woman conceived, and bare a son at that season that Elisha had said unto her, according to the time of life" (2 Kings 4:8-9).

When you connect with God first, He gives you the grace to network with His children all over the world, who will help you reach to a height where you cannot reach alone. Divine connection brings no sorrow with it, but rather provides true fellowship and fulfills desires and destiny.

> "¹⁶And the barrel of meal wasted not, neither did the cruse of oil fail, according to the word of the LORD, which he spake by Elijah. ¹⁷And it came to pass after these things, that the son of the woman, the mistress of

About family, God said that it is not good for a man to be alone. Two are better than one. Apart from marriage relationship, everyone needs someone to relate with, whether in the community, school, work, etc. Also, in our natural body, God sets members of the body to cooperate with each other.

> "*^{11}But all these worketh that one and the selfsame Spirit, dividing to every man severally as he will... ^{18}But now hath God set the members every one of them in the body, as it hath pleased him... ^{28}And God hath set some in the church, first apostles, secondarily prophets, thirdly teachers, after that miracles, then gifts of healings, helps, governments, diversities of tongues*" (1 Corinthians 12:11, 18).

We must prayerfully allow God to make choices for us. Our desires and aspirations in life must be in line with God's plans and purposes for God to guide us continually. To fully accomplish God's purposes for your life on earth, you must pray that God connects you to right people, who are prepared to help you.

> "*^{2}As they ministered to the Lord, and fasted, the Holy Ghost said, Separate me Barnabas and Saul for the work whereunto I have called them. ^{3}And when they had fasted and prayed, and laid their hands on them, they sent them away. ^{4}So they, being sent forth by the Holy Ghost, departed unto Seleucia; and from thence they sailed to Cyprus*" (Acts 13:2-4).

If you don't pray for divine connections, you are likely to keep meeting people, who will take you away from accomplishing God's will. It is a good thing to be born-again. But when you are not connected divinely with people and other things, you may be in danger of not fulfilling your destiny on earth.

> "*^{1}In the year that king Uzziah died I saw also the Lord sitting upon a throne, high and lifted up, and his train filled the temple. ^{2}Above it stood the seraphims: each one had six wings; with twain he covered his face, and*

with twain he covered his feet, and with twain he did fly. ³And one cried unto another, and said, Holy, holy, holy, is the LORD of hosts: the whole earth is full of his glory. ⁴And the posts of the door moved at the voice of him that cried, and the house was filled with smoke. ⁵Then said I, Woe is me! for I am undone; because I am a man of unclean lips, and I dwell in the midst of a people of unclean lips: for mine eyes have seen the King, the LORD of hosts. ⁶Then flew one of the seraphims unto me, having a live coal in his hand, which he had taken with the tongs from off the altar: ⁷And he laid it upon my mouth, and said, Lo, this hath touched thy lips; and thine iniquity is taken away, and thy sin purged. ⁸Also I heard the voice of the Lord, saying, Whom shall I send, and who will go for us? Then said I, Here am I; send me" (Isaiah 6:1-8).

You cannot afford to keep meeting with wrong people. Otherwise, you may never experience divine visitation that will turn your life around. You will be spiritually blinded and unable to know how Holy, powerful and glorious God is. You will be seeing the glory of men only and serving them instead of serving God. Praying for divine connections will help you to discover yourself, your destiny and tap directly from resources of heaven. Some people are deceived to believe they have arrived, only to be shocked seeing themselves down again.

Ensure that sin is not reigning in your success. Otherwise, you may be on your own; not being able to hear and answer God's calling for your life. When you connect with God, He will link you up with divine helpers and supporters, who will be competing to do you good instead of evil. Even when you are faced with battles, divine helpers will still come to your rescue.

"¹David therefore departed thence, and escaped to dullam: and when his brethren and all his father's house heard it, they went down thither to him. ²And every one that was in distress, and every one that was in debt, and every one that was discontented, gathered

> *themselves unto him; and he became a captain over them: and there were with him about four hundred men*" (1 Samuel 22:1-2).

> "⁵*Peter therefore was kept in prison: but prayer was made without ceasing of the church unto God for him. ⁶And when Herod would have brought him forth, the same night Peter was sleeping between two soldiers, bound with two chains: and the keepers before the door kept the prison. ⁷And, behold, the angel of the Lord came upon him, and a light shined in the prison: and he smote Peter on the side, and raised him up, saying, Arise up quickly. And his chains fell off from his hands*" (Acts 12:5-7).

Once you are rightly connected, divine helpers will locate and assist you, and will be ready to provide all you need.

> "²*And David sent forth a third part of the people under the hand of Joab, and a third part under the hand of Abishai the son of Zeruiah, Joab's brother, and a third part under the hand of Ittai the Gittite. And the king said unto the people, I will surely go forth with you myself also. ³But the people answered, Thou shalt not go forth: for if we flee away, they will not care for us; neither if half of us die, will they care for us: but now thou art worth ten thousand of us: therefore now it is better that thou succour us out of the city*" (2 Samuel 18:2-3).

> "¹⁴*And David was then in an hold, and the garrison of the Philistines was then in Beth–lehem. ¹⁵And David longed, and said, Oh that one would give me drink of the water of the well of Beth–lehem, which is by the gate! ¹⁶And the three mighty men brake through the host of the Philistines, and drew water out of the well of Beth–lehem, that was by the gate, and took it, and brought it to David: nevertheless he would not drink thereof, but poured it out unto the LORD. ¹⁷And he said, Be it far from me, O LORD, that I should do this: is not this the blood of the men that went in jeopardy of their lives? therefore he would not drink it. These*

things did these three mighty men" (2 Samuel 23:14-17).

Millions of people in the world today are involved in some wrong relationships and connections. Many others are married either to wrong partners, or are living in wrong places. Others are involved in wrong jobs and dealings with wrong people. These prayers are to help you pray targeted prayers, which bring results. May God answers your prayers, Amen.

PRAYER POINTS

1. Father Lord, arise and bless me with divine connections, in the name of Jesus.

2. Blood of Jesus, connect me with divine and true helpers, in the name of Jesus.

3. Holy Ghost fire, burn any evil mark in my life, in the name of Jesus.

4. Let the power of God link me up with heavenly angels, in the name of Jesus.

5. I receive power to be connected with people that matter, in the name of Jesus.

6. Any evil inscription in my life, spiritually or physically, catch fire, in the name of Jesus.

7. Let my life be empowered to attract unmerited favors, in the name of Jesus.

8. O Lord, connect me with people that will favor me exceedingly, in the name of Jesus.

9. Any curse that is separating me from people in authority, expire, in the name of Jesus.

10. I command every satanic label and stamp in my body to disappear, in the name of Jesus.

11. Blood of Jesus, beautify me to be accepted for good everywhere I go, in the name of Jesus.

12. Angels of the living God, take me to the right places at right times, in the name of Jesus.

13. O Lord, arise and ordain me to be respected and honored, in the name of Jesus.

14. I receive anointing to be sought for by great people, in the name of Jesus.

15. Father Lord, connect me to all manner of blessings forever, in Jesus name.

16. Every weapon of rejection prepared against me, catch fire, in the name of Jesus.

17. I blind every evil eye assigned to observe me for evil, in the name of Jesus.

18. Lord Jesus, connect me to people that are determined to help me succeed, in the name of Jesus.

19. I receive the grace of God to be connected to the great things of life, in the name of Jesus.

PRAYER TO PROSPER IN A FOREIGN LAND

It is usually not easy to be successful in foreign lands. As a foreigner, you are bound to experience certain limitations. But when God is with you, there is no limit to what you can achieve in a foreign land.

> "*¹The Word of the LORD came also unto me, saying, ²Thou shalt not take thee a wife, neither shalt thou have sons or daughters in this place. ³For thus saith the LORD concerning the sons and concerning the daughters that are born in this place, and concerning their mothers that bare them, and concerning their fathers that begat them in this land; ⁴They shall die of grievous deaths; they shall not be lamented; neither shall they be buried; but they shall be as dung upon the face of the earth: and they shall be consumed by the sword, and by famine; and their carcases shall be meat for the fowls of heaven, and for the beasts of the earth*" (Jeremiah 16:1-4).

It is also very important that you are born-again for God knows those who are His. It is always hard especially when one is not a born-again child. You may have difficulty contending forces of darkness from your place of birth or in the foreign land where you are. Demons have a way of communicating and handing people over to other territorial demons.

> "*¹⁵Then all the men which knew that their wives had burned incense unto other gods, and all the women that stood by, a great multitude, even all the people that dwelt in the land of Egypt, in Pathros, answered Jeremiah, saying, ¹⁶As for the word that thou hast spoken unto us in the name of the LORD, we will not hearken unto thee. ¹⁷But we will certainly do whatsoever thing goeth forth out of our own mouth, to burn incense unto the queen of heaven, and to pour*

out drink offerings unto her, as we have done, we, and our fathers, our kings, and our princes, in the cities of Judah, and in the streets of Jerusalem: for then had we plenty of victuals, and were well, and saw no evil. ^{18}But since we left off to burn incense to the queen of heaven, and to pour out drink offerings unto her, we have wanted all things, and have been consumed by the sword and by the famine" (Jeremiah 44:15-18).

You cannot enter into a covenant with environmental powers and prosper the way God has destined you to prosper.

"^{29}Or else how can one enter into a strong man's house, and spoil his goods, except he first bind the strong man? And then he will spoil his house" (Matthew 12:29).

You must avoid evil covenant, all manner of sin and devil's enticement. To prosper in a foreign land, you must deal with environmental forces of darkness.

PRAYER POINTS

1. Any evil force that has followed me to this land, scatter and die, in the name of Jesus.

2. Any evil power that is assigned to me in this country, be blinded to death, in the name of Jesus.

3. I break and loose myself from the power that fights strangers in this land, in the name of Jesus.

4. Every enemy of my mission in this land, be exposed and be disgraced, in the name of Jesus.

5. You, the gods of this land that has vowed to waste me, be wasted, in the name of Jesus.

6. Any evil sacrifice offered against me at my place of birth, expire, in the name of Jesus.

7. Wherever they are calling my name for evil, Lord Jesus, answer them, in the name of Jesus.

8. Any evil plan to limit my life, home or abroad, expire, in the name of Jesus.

9. Any evil arrow fired at me, backfire, in the name of Jesus.

10. O Lord, arise and bless my handiwork in this land, in the name of Jesus.

11. Let that power attacking my efforts in this land die, in the name of Jesus.

12. Every enemy of my progress, be disgraced, in the name of Jesus.

13. I refuse to cooperate with devil and his agents in this land, in the name of Jesus.

14. O Lord, give me true friends, neighbors and helpers, in the name of Jesus.

15. Let the power of God defend me in this land, in the name of Jesus.

16. Father Lord, make things easy for me in this land, in the name of Jesus.

17. Blood of Jesus, direct my steps in this land, in the name of Jesus.

18. No evil power shall rob me of my divine destiny, in the name of Jesus.

19. I command my divine destiny to rise and operate as God has ordained, in the name of Jesus.

20. Let forces of darkness militating against my life bow forever, in the name of Jesus.

21. Every arrow of confusion and all manner of problems fired at me, backfire, in the name of Jesus.

22. Any agent of devil empowered and directed to waste my life, be wasted, in the name of Jesus.

23. I refuse to partner with evil people, in the name of Jesus.

24. Let my God arise and take me to my place of prosperity and peace, in the name of Jesus.

25. Let God direct and empower people to help me, in the name of Jesus.

26. Any power assigned to re-arrange my destiny, be frustrated, in the name of Jesus.

27. Let every damage done to my relationship with my helpers be repaired, in the name of Jesus.

28. Father Lord, advertise Your goodness in me and help me to prosper, in the name of Jesus.

29. Let the light of the Almighty shine in my presence forever, in the name of Jesus.

30. I refuse to obey the devil or to do anything with his agents, in the name of Jesus.

31. Every inherited limitation in my life, be removed, in the name of Jesus.

32. O Lord, prosper me beyond the indigenes of this land, in the name of Jesus.

33. Father Lord, introduce me to the power that be and will be, in the name of Jesus.

34. Lord Jesus, better my relationship with people in this country, in the name of Jesus.

35. Let my stubborn enemies receive everlasting weakness and failures, in the name of Jesus.

36. Any Delilah and Jezebel anointing to destroy me, be destroyed, in the name of Jesus.

37. Any household enemy working hard to disgrace me, be disgraced, in the name of Jesus.

38. O Lord, feed me with the food of champions, in the name of Jesus.

39. O Lord, empower me and keep me in Your divine program, in the name of Jesus.

40. Any power creating problem for me, wherever you are, die, in the name of Jesus.

41. I block strange money, powers and things from coming in contact with me, in the name of Jesus.

42. Any satanic arrow shot for my sake, return back, in the name of Jesus.

43. I command the spirit of failure to avoid me forever, in the name of Jesus.

44. O Lord, deliver me from being involved in any criminal act, in the name of Jesus.

45. Any power assigned to hijack my star and destiny, die, in the name of Jesus.

46. Let destiny killers in this land fail woefully for my sake, in the name of Jesus.

47. Any kind of curse working in my life, expire, in the name of Jesus.

48. I break and loose myself from all manner of evil covenants, in the name of Jesus.

49. Any evil force contending with the angels of my blessing, die, in the name of Jesus.

50. Any satanic property inside my body, catch fire, in the name of Jesus.

51. Any problem swallowing my money, die, in the name of Jesus.

52. Any immigration problem distracting my attention, die, in the name of Jesus.

53. Any satanic minister, ministering against me, be disgraced, in the name of Jesus.

54. Any power that is affecting my breakthrough, I terminate your existence, in the name of Jesus.

55. Let all forces of darkness, diverting my efforts, die in shame, in the name of Jesus.

56. Any relationship assigned to put me to shame or trouble, be terminated, in the name of Jesus.

57. Let my angels of blessing appear and bless me, in the name of Jesus.

58. Any demon with a vow to disgrace me, fail woefully, in the name of Jesus.

59. I command any vagabond anointing upon me to be broken, in the name of Jesus.

60. O Lord, help me to buy a home, a car and all that will make my life comfortable in this land, in the name of Jesus.

61. I disgrace every trace of poverty in my life, in the name of Jesus.

62. Any witch or wizard targeting my life, be frustrated, in the name of Jesus.

63. Every good thing devil has arrested in my life, be released, in the name of Jesus.

64. O Lord, restart Your project in my life now, in the name of Jesus.

65. Let the mercy, grace and power of God be doubled in my life, in the name of Jesus.

66. You my personal stronghold, collapse, in the name of Jesus.

67. Let all my problems receive double destruction, in the name of Jesus.

68. O Lord, deliver me from court cases, police cases, and hospital and immigration cases, in the name of Jesus.

69. Let my problems receive double and bitter defeats, in the name of Jesus.

PRAYER TO RECOVER LOST BUSINESSES

Satan comes to steal. That is his ministry. However, there are demons on earth referred to as agents of lost. They are responsible for most great losses on earth. If you don't know how to deal with them, they are capable of messing your life up and forcing tears out of your eyes. These evil agents have used their powers to bring down many great and destined generals, tycoons and billionaires.

> "*^{10}The thief cometh not, but for to steal, and to kill, and to destroy: I am come that they might have life, and that they might have it more abundantly*" (John 10:10).

> "*^{25}But while men slept, his enemy came and sowed tares among the wheat, and went his way. ^{26}But when the blade was sprung up, and brought forth fruit, then appeared the tares also*" (Matthew 13:25-26).

> "*^{16}And it came to pass, as we went to prayer, a certain damsel possessed with a spirit of divination met us, which brought her masters much gain by soothsaying... ^{19}And when her masters saw that the hope of their gains was gone, they caught Paul and Silas, and drew them into the marketplace unto the rulers*" (Acts 16:16, 19).

The activities of these demons are real. They are often referred to as spiritual criminals, destiny quenchers and soul traders. They are capable of depriving people of their rights, benefits and entitlements. They put a mark of hatred, rejection and vagabond spirits on some of their victims, who find it difficult to achieve greatness or fulfill their destinies. But God has given us power over these wicked forces.

> "*^{18}Verily I say unto you, Whatsoever ye shall bind on earth shall be bound in heaven: and whatsoever ye*

shall loose on earth shall be loosed in heaven. ¹⁹Again I say unto you, That if two of you shall agree on earth as touching anything that they shall ask, it shall be done for them of my Father which is in heaven" (Matthew 18:18-19).

"²⁸Thou shalt also decree a thing, and it shall be established unto thee: and the light shall shine upon thy ways" (Job 22:28).

The prayers in this program are designed to target these demonic forces. You need to come against them with the spirit of *"If I perish I perish."*

"¹And the sons of the prophets said unto Elisha, Behold now, the place where we dwell with thee is too strait for us. ²Let us go, we pray thee, unto Jordan, and take thence every man a beam, and let us make us a place there, where we may dwell. And he answered, Go ye. ³And one said, Be content, I pray thee, and go with thy servants. And he answered, I will go. ⁴So he went with them. And when they came to Jordan, they cut down wood. ⁵But as one was felling a beam, the axe head fell into the water: and he cried, and said, Alas, master! for it was borrowed. ⁶And the man of God said, Where fell it? And he shewed him the place. And he cut down a stick, and cast it in thither; and the iron did swim. ⁷Therefore said he, Take it up to thee. And he put out his hand, and took it" (2 Kings 6:1-7).

When you pray fervently, there is nothing lost that cannot be recovered. Lazarus recovered his life after four days in the tomb because his sisters prayed. Paul recovered his sight because he prayed. A marine fish vomited Jonah because he prayed. When you pray, God surely answers.

PRAYER POINTS

1. I take back every good thing my ancestors handed over to devil, in the name of Jesus.

2. O Lord, arise and help me to recover all that I have given to devil, in the name of Jesus.

3. Any evil promise that has robbed me of my greatness, I renounce you, in the name of Jesus.

4. Blood of Jesus, speak me back into my inheritance today, in the name of Jesus.

5. I recover double every good thing devil has stolen from me, in the name of Jesus.

6. Every good thing I have lost in my dreams, I recover you double, in the name of Jesus.

7. Let the angels of God fight for me and recover all my loss, in the name of Jesus.

8. I command my finances in the hand of the enemy to be recovered, in the name of Jesus.

9. Any man, woman or power that has stolen my destiny, restore it now, in the name of Jesus.

10. I command all that are in possession of my prosperity to restore them now, in the name of Jesus.

11. You, my buried potentials, I command you to resurrect, in the name of Jesus.

12. Any power of darkness that has arrested my star, release it by force, in the name of Jesus.

13. Every enemy of my breakthrough, die, in the name of Jesus.

14. Every yoke hindering my deliverance, beak by fire, in the name of Jesus.

15. O Lord, arise and perfect Your deliverance in my life, in the name of Jesus.

16. Blood of Jesus, speak my health out of demonic captivities, in the name of Jesus.

17. Any satanic case holding me down, break by fire, in the name of Jesus.

18. Any satanic agent sitting upon my joy and peace, be unseated by death, in the name of Jesus.

19. Every good thing I have lost to the water spirits, I recover them double, in the name of Jesus.

20. Father Lord, take me to my Promised Land, in the name of Jesus.

21. Everything that will help me to fulfill my destiny and make heaven, I receive you now, in the name of Jesus.

PRAYER TO RECOVER A LOST JOB

No matter what you have lost in life, if you abide in Christ and prayerfully refuse to bow or negotiate with the devil, you will recover all that you have lost.

> "*[1]And the sons of the prophets said unto Elisha, Behold now, the place where we dwell with thee is too strait for us. [2]Let us go, we pray thee, unto Jordan, and take thence every man a beam, and let us make us a place there, where we may dwell. And he answered, Go ye. [3]And one said, Be content, I pray thee, and go with thy servants. And he answered, I will go. [4]So he went with them. And when they came to Jordan, they cut down wood. [5]But as one was felling a beam, the axe head fell into the water: and he cried, and said, Alas, master! for it was borrowed. [6]And the man of God said, Where fell it? And he shewed him the place. And he cut down a stick, and cast it in thither; and the iron did swim. [7]Therefore said he, Take it up to thee. And he put out his hand, and took it*" (2 Kings 6:1-7).

If you lost your job and you want it back, all you need to pray for is to know whether you have not overstayed. If God is not the one that took or allow the job to be taken to give you a better one, you can recover your job.

> "*[38]Jesus therefore again groaning in himself cometh to the grave. It was a cave, and a stone lay upon it. [39]Jesus said, Take ye away the stone. Martha, the sister of him that was dead, saith unto him, Lord, by this time he stinketh: for he hath been dead four days. [40]Jesus saith unto her, Said I not unto thee, that, if thou wouldest believe, thou shouldest see the glory of God? [41]Then they took away the stone from the place where the dead was laid. And Jesus lifted up his eyes, and said, Father, I thank thee that thou hast heard me. [42]And I knew that thou hearest me always: but because*

of the people which stand by I said it, that they may believe that thou hast sent me. [43]And when he thus had spoken, he cried with a loud voice, Lazarus, come forth. [44]And he that was dead came forth, bound hand and foot with grave clothes: and his face was bound about with a napkin. Jesus saith unto them, Loose him, and let him go" (John 11:38-44).

No witch, wizard, grave or the worst evil altar can keep back all that a prayerful right living believer has lost.

"[32]He that spared not his own Son, but delivered him up for us all, how shall he not with him also freely give us all things?" (Romans 8:32).

Pray and believe God for total recovery (*See also* 1 Samuel 30:1-31).

PRAYER POINTS

1. I claim back my lost job by force, in the name of Jesus.

2. Any satanic angel that has stolen my job, release it by force, in the name of Jesus.

3. Every satanic embargo placed upon the recovery of my job, be lifted, in the name of Jesus.

4. Every aggression directed against the recovery of my job, be dismantled, in the name of Jesus.

5. Every door closed against the recovery of my job, open by force, in the name of Jesus.

6. Any evil personality sitting upon my job, be unseated by death, in the name of Jesus.

7. Every evil decree passed against my job, be reversed, in the name of Jesus in Jesus name.

8. Any open threat to keep me out of job, be frustrated, in the name of Jesus.

9. Blood of Jesus, destroy every mark of hatred and rejection against my job, in the name of Jesus.

10. Holy Ghost fire, burn to ashes any evil power sitting upon my job, in the name of Jesus.

11. Every demonic antagonism against my job, be disgraced, in the name of Jesus.

12. Blood of Jesus, frustrate every satanic strife against my job, in the name of Jesus.

13. I command confusion that will restore my job back to manifest, in the name of Jesus.

14. Let my enemies make costly mistakes that will favor me, in the name of Jesus.

15. Every demonic opinion against my life, be rejected, in the name of Jesus.

16. Every unprofitable action against my job, be neglected, in the name of Jesus.

17. Father Lord, remove every unprofitable controversies against my job, in the name of Jesus.

18. I push away every demonic logic against my job, in the name of Jesus.

19. Let every evil gathering against my job scatter to my favor, in the name of Jesus.

20. I command every satanic judgment against my job to be rendered null and void, in the name of Jesus.

I withdraw every access that Satan has gained over my job, in the name of Jesus.

PRAYER TO RECOVER ALL YOUR LOSS

So many people have lost great things in their lives. Usually, when you refuse to fight in order to regain your loss, you will continue loose more things that are valuable. Even believers, who have failed to pray for their recoveries, have continued to count more losses. But through prayers, you will surely recover all your losses in the name of Jesus, Amen.

> "*¹And the sons of the prophets said unto Elisha, Behold now, the place where we dwell with thee is too strait for us. ²Let us go, we pray thee, unto Jordan, and take thence every man a beam, and let us make us a place there, where we may dwell. And he answered, Go ye. ³And one said, Be content, I pray thee, and go with thy servants. And he answered, I will go. ⁴So he went with them. And when they came to Jordan, they cut down wood. ⁵But as one was felling a beam, the axe head fell into the water: and he cried, and said, Alas, master! for it was borrowed. ⁶And the man of God said, Where fell it? And he shewed him the place. And he cut down a stick, and cast it in thither; and the iron did swim. ⁷Therefore said he, Take it up to thee. And he put out his hand, and took it*" (2 Kings 6:1-7).

Evil altars, which exist in the land, seas and the heavenlies, have captured and confiscated destines of millions of people. If you choose to ignore the activities of these altars, you may not enjoy your life even as a Christian. Destinies of many great people have been captured and are being used for the benefit of other people.

> "*¹⁶And it came to pass, as we went to prayer, a certain damsel possessed with a spirit of divination met us, which brought her masters much gain by soothsaying... ¹⁹And when her masters saw that the hope of their gains was gone, they caught Paul and*

Silas, and drew them into the marketplace unto the rulers" (Acts 16:16, 19).

Pray that your destiny and greatness will leave the camp of the enemy and rejoin you today. You can still recover every good thing you have ever lost in life in the name of Jesus, Amen.

PRAYER POINTS

1. O Lord, empower me to recover the good things I have lost in life, in the name of Jesus.

2. Anything my family idol has stolen from me, I recover you double, in the name of Jesus.

3. I take back all that my ancestors handed over to devil, in the name of Jesus.

4. I recover by force all that I have lost to water spirits, in the name of Jesus.

5. Let all that witches and wizards stole from me begin to return, in the name of Jesus.

6. Blood of Jesus, recover all the good things that has left my life, in the name of Jesus.

7. I make a way for the returning of my lost blessings, in the name of Jesus.

8. All that evil agents stole from me, be restored double, in the name of Jesus.

9. I command my hijacked destiny to return by force, in the name of Jesus.

10. I take back all my financial loses, in the name of Jesus.

11. Let all my lost helpers find their way back into my life, in the name of Jesus.

12. Everything that makes me happy, stolen by the devil, I recover you, in the name of Jesus.

13. I stretch forth my hand and I recover all my lost blessings, in the name of Jesus.

14. Every good thing that sin has handed over to the devil, I recover you now, in the name of Jesus.

15. Ancient of days, help me to recover my stolen miracles and blessings, in the name of Jesus.

16. Any evil place that is hiding my lost breakthrough, release them by force, in the name of Jesus.

17. Every good thing that spiritual armed robbers stole from me, come back now, in the name of Jesus.

18. Let the hand of God enter into every creature and retrieve my lost blessings, in the name of Jesus.

19. Any of my blessings and God's promises trapped in the camp of devil, I recover you now, in the name of Jesus.

20. Angels of the living God, go into the land of the living and the dead and bring back my blessings, in the name of Jesus.

PRAYER TO REVIVE COLLAPSED OR COLLAPSING BUSINESS

Businesses all over the world are collapsing. Many organizations are facing challenges that threaten their existence. Economists and experts have found themselves in unexpected dilemma. They call it global economic meltdown. But let us be clear here; <u>the system that is collapsing is global Babylonian economic system.</u> God's economic system thrives. God's people are doing great exploits all over the world. Therefore, this is the right time to move your businesses into God's system to witness divine restoration.

> "*¹And it came to pass, that, as the people pressed upon him to hear the Word of God, he stood by the lake of Gennesaret, ²And saw two ships standing by the lake: but the fishermen were gone out of them, and were washing their nets. ³And he entered into one of the ships, which was Simon's, and prayed him that he would thrust out a little from the land. And he sat down, and taught the people out of the ship*" (Luke 5:1-3).

That's exactly what Peter and others did at the lake of Gennesaret. They abandoned their ships; folded their business and were washing their nets. These were well-known professional fishermen, but they failed until Christ showed up.

> "*⁴Now when he had left speaking, he said unto Simon, Launch out into the deep, and let down your nets for a draught. ⁵And Simon answering said unto him, Master, we have toiled all the night, and have taken nothing: nevertheless at thy word I will let down the net. ⁶And when they had this done, they inclosed a great multitude of fishes: and their net brake. ⁷And*

they beckoned unto their partners, which were in the other ship, that they should come and help them. And they came, and filled both the ships, so that they began to sink" (Luke 5:4-7).

That is why when you repent, confess, forsake your sins and invite Christ into your life, your businesses revive and continue to blossom. What then are you waiting for?

PRAYER POINTS

1. Any power pulling my businesses down, die, in the name of Jesus.

2. O Lord, deliver my business from total collapse, in the name of Jesus.

3. Let the forces of darkness against me business scatter, in the name of Jesus.

4. Blood of Jesus, speak life to my business today, in the name of Jesus.

5. Any satanic padlock on my business, break, in the name of Jesus.

6. O Lord, arise and take my business to the next level, in the name of Jesus.

7. O Lord, visit my business with opened door for prosperity, in the name of Jesus.

8. Any evil hand upon my business, dry up by force, in the name of Jesus.

9. Any power attacking my business, be disgraced, in the name of Jesus.

10. Any personal stronghold built against this business, collapse, in the name of Jesus.

11. Any evil deposit on my business, catch fire, burn to ashes, in the name of Jesus.

12. Any occult arrow fired at this business, backfire, in the name of Jesus.

13. Any satanic traffic into my business, be removed by force, in the name of Jesus.

14. Any evil action taken against my business, catch fire, in the name of Jesus.

15. Any evil priest ordained for the sake of my business, be disgraced, in the name of Jesus.

16. Any evil advertisement against my business, be stopped, in the name of Jesus.

17. Any rage of poverty against my business, catch fire, in the name of Jesus.

18. Blood of Jesus, resurrect my business today, in the name of Jesus.

19. Any satanic poison in my business, expire, in the name of Jesus.

20. Any arrow of fruitless efforts upon my business, backfire, in the name of Jesus.

21. Any evil personality, manipulating my business, be manipulated, in the name of Jesus.

22. Any counterfeit money in my business, be removed, in the name of Jesus.

23. Any household wickedness targeting my business, be removed, in the name of Jesus.

24. Any evil program going on against my business, stop, in the name of Jesus.

25. Any traffic warden diverting customers away from my business, die, in the name of Jesus.

26. Any evil prophecy made upon my business, fail, in the name of Jesus.

27. Any power that has bewitched my business, release it now, in the name of Jesus.

28. Let business terminating demons targeting my business be terminated, in the name of Jesus.

29. Every unprofitable load upon my business, drop by force, in the name of Jesus.

30. Any power that has seized the progress of my business, release it and die, in the name of Jesus.

31. I command all shame distributors on my business to carry their shame and go, in the name of Jesus.

32. Any angel of business failure assigned to my businesses, be exposed and disgraced, in the name of Jesus.

33. Any hidden oppressor against my business, be exposed and disgraced, in the name of Jesus.

34. Any power that has caged my business, release it and die, in the name of Jesus.

35. Any evil arrest of my business, be frustrated, in the name of Jesus.

PRAYER TO REVOKE EVIL DECREES

A decree is an order with the power of legislation issued by a ruler or other person or group with authority. Evil decrees are not issues to be handled lightly or joked with. They are decrees with intent to harm or end life. Mordecai warned Esther about an evil decree and Esther was wise enough to take urgent steps to terminate the decree. Otherwise, thousands of Jews would have lost their lives.

> "*[12]Then were the king's scribes called on the thirteenth day of the first month, and there was written according to all that Haman had commanded unto the king's lieutenants, and to the governors that were over every province, and to the rulers of every people of every province according to the writing thereof, and to every people after their language; in the name of king Ahasuerus was it written, and sealed with the king's ring. [13]And the letters were sent by posts into all the king's provinces, to destroy, to kill, and to cause to perish, all Jews, both young and old, little children and women, in one day, even upon the thirteenth day of the twelfth month, which is the month Adar, and to take the spoil of them for a prey. [14]The copy of the writing for a commandment to be given in every province was published unto all people, that they should be ready against that day*" (Esther 3:12-14).

Evil decree is capable of consuming an entire nation. It can reduce its victims to slaves and unproductive or useless elements. Many young people have lost their lives to evil decrees. It rendered many adult useless and stopped great people.

> "*[14]The copy of the writing for a commandment to be given in every province was published unto all people, that they should be ready against that day. [15]The posts went out, being hastened by the king's commandment,*

and the decree was given in Shushan the palace. And the king and Haman sat down to drink; but the city Shushan was perplexed" (Esther 3:14-15).

"²⁷And Joshua made them that day hewers of wood and drawers of water for the congregation, and for the altar of the LORD, even unto this day, in the place which he should choose" (Joshua 9:27).

An evil decree can end the lives of thousands of people and their properties confiscated. It can wipe out an entire nation or city. You need to take this program seriously because many peoples' survival depends on it. Esther and Mordecai decided to die than to allow an evil decree become effective. They prayed and fasted as they never did before and God reversed the evil for their sakes.

PRAYER POINTS

1. Father Lord, thank You for Your words are final, in the name of Jesus.

2. O Lord, reverse any evil decree made against me, in the name of Jesus.

3. Any evil utterance ever said against me, be revoked by force, in the name of Jesus.

4. Blood of Jesus, speak destruction to every evil word spoken against me, in the name of Jesus.

5. Any power sponsoring evil statements against me, be disgraced, in the name of Jesus.

6. I break and loose myself from evil utterances by anyone living or dead, in the name of Jesus.

7. Holy Ghost fire, revoke every evil decree against my destiny, in the name of Jesus.

8. Let the handwriting of devil against me be rubbed off now, in the name of Jesus.

9. Let the anger of God destroy every evil imagination against me, in the name of Jesus.

10. Every satanic opinion against me, be rejected, in the name of Jesus.

11. Every curse placed upon me, expire, in the name of Jesus.

12. Every curse issued against me by anyone living or dead, I revoke you, in the name of Jesus.

13. I walk out from consequences of evil decrees, in the name of Jesus.

14. I break and loose myself from family or generational bondage, in the name of Jesus.

15. I command every satanic decision to become invalid, in the name of Jesus.

16. Every evil judgment against me, be revoked by force, in the name of Jesus.

17. I walk out from curses laid on me, in the name of Jesus.

18. I recover every blessing the enemy has diverted from me through curses, in the name of Jesus.

19. Any evil prayer against me, fail, in the name of Jesus.

20. Any evil statement ever made against me consciously, let the enemy be wasted instead, in the name of Jesus.

21. Let the hand of God take away all my problems today, in the name of Jesus.

Mon 2/23/15

PRAYER TO RISE FROM DEFEAT

God's purpose for your life is not defeat. It is of peace and not of evil; to give you an expected end (*See* Jeremiah 11:29). Only God has the power to do whatever He wills to do anytime and for anyone. And He wants you to succeed. May God grant you the change you need through your prayers.

> "⁹*And Jabez was more honorable than his brethren: and his mother called his name Jabez, saying, Because I bare him with sorrow.* ¹⁰*And Jabez called on the God of Israel, saying, Oh that thou wouldest bless me indeed, and enlarge my coast, and that thine hand might be with me, and that thou wouldest keep me from evil, that it may not grieve me! And God granted him that which he requested*" (1 Chronicles 4:9-10).

> "⁶*Be careful for nothing; but in every thing by prayer and supplication with thanksgiving let your requests be made known unto God*" (Philippians 4:6).

Barrenness defeated Hannah for so many years, but she refused to submit to it. She went to the house of God and God took her away from defeat to victory. The judgment of death was passed against Hezekiah, but he rejected it and turned to God in prayers. What defeats have you accepted in your life? Why don't you borrow a leaf from Hannah and Hezekiah and reject defeat? Now, is the time you turn to God in prayers for victory. And He will see you through in the name of Jesus, Amen.

> "¹*In those days was Hezekiah sick unto death. And Isaiah the prophet the son of Amoz came unto him, and said unto him, Thus saith the LORD, Set thine house in order: for thou shalt die, and not live.* ²*Then Hezekiah turned his face toward the wall, and prayed unto the LORD,* ³*And said, Remember now, O LORD, I beseech thee, how I have walked before thee in*

truth and with a perfect heart, and have done that which is good in thy sight. And Hezekiah wept sore. ⁴Then came the word of the LORD to Isaiah, saying, ⁵Go, and say to Hezekiah, Thus saith the LORD, the God of David thy father, I have heard thy prayer, I have seen thy tears: behold, I will add unto thy days fifteen years" (Isaiah 38:1-5).

God is waiting for your prayers. If you are a sinner, you need to repent and pray for victory. Daniel was thrown into the lion's dens, but he came out alive without any hurt. No covenant child of God is destined to die in defeat.

PRAYER POINTS

1. Any evil action that is keeping me below my standard, be roasted by fire, in the name of Jesus.

2. Let the destroying flood of God carry away all my defeats, in the name of Jesus.

3. Blood of Jesus, speak me out of every defeat in life, in the name of Jesus.

4. O Lord, arise and promote me everywhere I go, in the name of Jesus.

5. Power to rise and shine, possess me by force, in the name of Jesus.

6. Let my complete deliverance from defeat come from above, in the name of Jesus.

7. Any evil covenant keeping me out of victory, break, in the name of Jesus.

8. Any curse attacking my advancement, expire forever, in the name of Jesus.

9. I command the spirit of failure in my life to be cut off, in the name of Jesus.

10. Let the prosperity that will swallow the spirit of poverty overrun me, in the name of Jesus.

11. Any evil traffic blocking my victory, be dismantled, in the name of Jesus.

12. Any witch or wizard that is harvesting my efforts, be disgraced, in the name of Jesus.

13. Any power, caging my destiny, release it by force, in the name of Jesus.

14. Father Lord, anoint me to rise and shine always, in the name of Jesus.

15. I raise my head up and remain progressive forever, in the name of Jesus.

16. Any evil weapon designed to pull me down, catch fire, in the name of Jesus.

17. Any satanic agent anointed to steal my victory, be disgraced, in the name of Jesus.

18. Let my prosperity grow on daily basis, in the name of Jesus.

19. I command my progress anointing to increase every moment, in the name of Jesus.

PRAYER TO SEARCH AND FIND A JOB

God's Word declared that when you ask, you receive; seek, you find; knock, it will be opened unto. Therefore, when you seek for a worthy job, believing in your heart that God's Word is true, you will surely receive on.

> *"Ask, and it shall be given you; seek, and ye shall find; knock, and it shall be opened unto you: For everyone that asketh reciveth; and he that seeketh findeth; and to him that knocketh it shall be opened. Or what man is thereof you, whom if his son asks bread, will he give him a stone? Or if he ask a fish, will he give him a serpent? If ye then, bring evil, know how to give good gifts unto your children, how much more shall your father which is in heaven give good things to them that ask him"* (Matthew 7:7-11).

When you trust for a job, He will bless you. Prayer of faith is very effective. By grace, you will get the job of your dream in any part of the world. You must have faith because is the key that unlocks the door of heaven's gate to get anything you want.

> *"^{14}And when they were come to the multitude, there came to him a certain man, kneeling down to him, and saying, ^{15}Lord, have mercy on my son: for he is lunatick, and sore vexed: for ofttimes he falleth into the fire, and oft into the water. ^{16}And I brought him to thy disciples, and they could not cure him. ^{17}Then Jesus answered and said, O faithless and perverse generation, how long shall I be with you? how long shall I suffer you? Bring him hither to me. ^{18}And Jesus rebuked the devil; and he departed out of him: and the child was cured from that very hour. ^{19}Then came the disciples to Jesus apart, and said, Why could not we cast him out? ^{20}And Jesus said unto them, Because of your unbelief: for verily I say unto you, If ye have faith*

as a grain of mustard seed, ye shall say unto this mountain, Remove hence to yonder place; and it shall remove; and nothing shall be impossible unto you" (Matthew 17:14-20).

"⁵If any of you lack wisdom, let him ask of God, that giveth to all men liberally, and upbraideth not; and it shall be given him. ⁶But let him ask in faith, nothing wavering. For he that wavereth is like a wave of the sea driven with the wind and tossed. ⁷For let not that man think that he shall receive any thing of the Lord. ⁸A double minded man is unstable in all his ways" (James 1:5-8).

Fear, unbelief, doubt and discouragement are opposites of faith. God is more willing to give us anything than we are willing to receive. Whenever there is failure in receiving answers to prayers, it is possible you are praying out of the will of God for your life. If you are searching for a job, pray these targeted prayers and trust God for a good job.

You must not allow the devil or his agents to keep you out of job. Believers, who know their rights, persevere until the end and prayerfully pray themselves into right offices like Daniel and his three friends. God is able also to give you the wisdom to own a business of your choice. Ask Him, and then trust Him too.

PRAYER POINTS

1. Father Lord, arise and help me to get a good job, in the name of Jesus.

2. I command my application for new job to be honored, in the name of Jesus.

3. O Lord, help me to satisfy the demands of my employers, in the name of Jesus.

4. Any obstacle hindering me from getting a better job, die, in the name of Jesus.

5. Lord Jesus, direct my steps to where I can get a good job, in the name of Jesus.

6. I break every curse in my life preventing me from getting great jobs, in the name of Jesus.

7. I command evil personalities hindering me to be disgraced, in the name of Jesus.

8. Lord, fill me with Your wisdom to pass my job interview, in the name of Jesus.

9. Anointing to perform excellently for the best job, possess me, in the name of Jesus.

10. Any counter movement to stop me from getting a new job, die, in the name of Jesus.

11. Lord Jesus, make me acceptable for a new job, in the name of Jesus.

12. Father Lord, give me divine direction for a much better job offer, in the name of Jesus.

13. Let the activities of devil preventing me from getting a better job die, in the name of Jesus.

14. Any strong man that has vowed to block me, fall down and die, in the name of Jesus.

15. Every agent of disappointment assigned to frustrate me, fail woefully, in the name of Jesus.

16. I receive power for maximum performance for the best job, in the name of Jesus.

17. Any activity of household wickedness against me, be paralyzed, in the name of Jesus.

18. Blood of Jesus, speak me into the job of my dreams, in the name of Jesus.

19. I receive the job that will help fulfill my destiny, in the name of Jesus.

PRAYER TO STOP DETERMINED ENEMIES

Satan is determined to waste peoples' destinies at all cost through problems and calamities. You cannot afford to play down some calamities or take them lightly. Otherwise, you they consume you before you know it.

> "*¹²And when it was day, certain of the Jews banded together, and bound themselves under a curse, saying that they would neither eat nor drink till they had killed Paul. ¹³And they were more than forty, which had made this conspiracy. ¹⁴And they came to the chief priests and elders, and said, We have bound ourselves under a great curse, that we will eat nothing until we have slain Paul*" (Acts 23:12-14).

> "*¹And Saul, yet breathing out threatenings and slaughter against the disciples of the Lord, went unto the high priest, ²And desired of him letters to Damascus to the synagogues, that if he found any of this way, whether they were men or women, he might bring them bound unto Jerusalem*" (Acts 9:1-2).

In Paul's day, certain Jews, who were under the influence of the spirit of death and suicide, bound themselves under a curse not to eat nor drink until they have killed Paul. As it was in those days, so it is still today and even worst in most places. There are demons and human agents, who have vowed never to rest until they have finished your life, business or your health. You don't want to take these firmness lightly. If you refuse to do something about it, you may not survive these evil plots.

> "*⁵And the LORD came down to see the city and the tower, which the children of men builded. ⁶And the LORD said, Behold, the people is one, and they have all one language; and this they begin to do: and now*

nothing will be restrained from them, which they have imagined to do" (Genesis 11:5-6).

"¹It came to pass after this also, that the children of Moab, and the children of Ammon, and with them other beside the Ammonites, came against Jehoshaphat to battle. ²Then there came some that told Jehoshaphat, saying, There cometh a great multitude against thee from beyond the sea on this side Syria; and, behold, they be in Hazazon–tamar, which is En–gedi. ³And Jehoshaphat feared, and set himself to seek the LORD, and proclaimed a fast throughout all Judah" (2 Chronicles 20:1-3).

God knows that if your enemies were allowed without any challenge, they would have their way. Jehoshaphat feared his enemies, but did not stop there. He set himself to seek the Lord for help against his determined enemies.

"⁹O Belteshazzar, master of the magicians, because I know that the spirit of the holy gods is in thee, and no secret troubleth thee, tell me the visions of my dream that I have seen, and the interpretation thereof... ¹⁵Nevertheless leave the stump of his roots in the earth, even with a band of iron and brass, in the tender grass of the field; and let it be wet with the dew of heaven, and let his portion be with the beasts in the grass of the earth: ¹⁶Let his heart be changed from man's, and let a beast's heart be given unto him; and let seven times pass over him. ¹⁷This matter is by the decree of the watchers, and the demand by the word of the holy ones: to the intent that the living may know that the most High ruleth in the kingdom of men, and giveth it to whomsoever he will, and setteth up over it the basest of men" (Daniel 4:9, 15-17).

When you fall short of challenging your enemies, they will attack you from every direction with whatever they can lay their hands on. Joshua challenged the sun and moon. Jacob prayed all night and his name was changed. Hannah challenged barrenness and it bowed out. What is it that you are afraid to challenge?

PRAYER POINTS

1. Every determined enemy of my life, your time is up, die, in the name of Jesus.

2. Any aggressive altar militating against my destiny, scatter, in the name of Jesus.

3. Any power attacking my family, I cut off your existence, in the name of Jesus.

4. Any stubborn yoke of poverty in my life, break, in the name of Jesus.

5. O Lord, arise and destroy every unrepentant enemy of my life, in the name of Jesus.

6. Any ancestral covenant in my life, break to pieces, in the name of Jesus.

7. I break and loose myself from destructive curses, in the name of Jesus.

8. Blood of Jesus, flow into my foundation, in the name of Jesus.

9. Any ghost on assignment to terminate my life, be frustrated, in the name of Jesus.

10. Any evil decree against my life, be reversed by force, in the name of Jesus.

11. Any evil judgment pronounced against my life, I reject you, in the name of Jesus.

12. Any evil determined enemy that has vowed to kill me, die, in the name of Jesus.

13. Any witch or wizard, militating against my soul, fail, in the name of Jesus.

14. O Lord, arise and kill all my killers, in the name of Jesus.

15. Any evil pregnancy against my soul, be aborted, in the name of Jesus.

16. Lord Jesus, deliver me from every evil forces, in the name of Jesus.

17. You, the strongman over my life, die by force, in the name of Jesus.

18. Any stronghold built against my life, collapse, in the name of Jesus.

19. Any enemy in the dark room of my life, die, in the name of Jesus.

20. Father Lord, arise and protect me from enemies of my soul, in the name of Jesus.

PRAYER TO SUCCEED WHERE OTHERS ARE FAILING

It will take the grace of God to succeed where many are failing. That's why Jesus said, *"With men this is impossible; but with God all things are possible"* (Matthew 19:26). If you are going to make real progress and difference in this life to advance the kingdom of God, you need to trust God to succeed where others are failing. Otherwise, succeeding where others are succeeding does not make any difference.

"19Then was the secret revealed unto Daniel in a night vision. Then Daniel blessed the God of heaven" (Daniel 2:19).

"9And after him was Eleazar the son of Dodo the Ahohite, one of the three mighty men with David, when they defied the Philistines that were there gathered together to battle, and the men of Israel were gone away: 10He arose, and smote the Philistines until his hand was weary, and his hand clave unto the sword: and the LORD wrought a great victory that day; and the people returned after him only to spoil. 11And after him was Shammah the son of Agee the Hararite. And the Philistines were gathered together into a troop, where was a piece of ground full of lentiles: and the people fled from the Philistines. 12But he stood in the midst of the ground, and defended it, and slew the Philistines: and the LORD wrought a great victory. 13And three of the thirty chief went down, and came to David in the harvest time unto the cave of Adullam: and the troop of the Philistines pitched in the valley of Rephaim. 14And David was then in an hold, and the garrison of the Philistines was then in Beth–lehem. 15And David longed, and said, Oh that one would give me drink of the water of the well of

> *Beth–lehem, which is by the gate!* ¹⁶*And the three mighty men brake through the host of the Philistines, and drew water out of the well of Beth–lehem, that was by the gate, and took it, and brought it to David: nevertheless he would not drink thereof, but poured it out unto the LORD"* ([2 Samuel 23:9-16](#)).

God is searching for people He will use to liberate the world. He is looking for people, who will make real differences. Our generation needs men and women of grace, who have matured spiritually, saved, clothed with humility and compassionate as Jesus. Only such men and women can follow God's Word no matter the consequence.

God is looking for people, who will manifest his DNA to the world; courageous men and women, who can champion life of purity and saintly purpose. He is searching for people He can empower to succeed where others have failed woefully. If you are ready, pray these prayers of excellence.

PRAYER POINTS

1. Any power keeping me out of my place of blessing, release me and die, in the name of Jesus.

2. I walk out of evil cells forever by force, in the name of Jesus.

3. O Lord, empower me to succeed in this life, in the name of Jesus.

4. You my prosperity, arise and locate me by force, in the name of Jesus.

5. Enemies of my breakthrough, I cut off your heads, in the name of Jesus.

6. Every agent of failure in my life, I reject you completely, in the name of Jesus.

7. Any witch or wizard bewitching people in this place, fail for my sake, in the name of Jesus.

8. Any seed of failure planted in my life, die by force, in the name of Jesus.

9. Angels of the living God, empower me to succeed where many failed, in the name of Jesus.

10. Any satanic program against my success, be terminated, in the name of Jesus.

11. Heavenly father, send Your help from above, in the name of Jesus.

12. Any evil chain tying me down in bondage, break, in the name of Jesus.

13. Power to succeed exceedingly, possess me, in the name of Jesus.

14. Anointing to make progress where many have failed, possess me, in the name of Jesus.

15. Any chain of backwardness holding me down, break to pieces, in the name of Jesus.

16. O Lord, send my angel of blessing from heaven to help me, in the name of Jesus.

17. Any evil vow made to stop my progress, expire and fail, in the name of Jesus.

18. I receive power to succeed where others are failing, in the name of Jesus.

From Prayer Retreat pg 143

Any evil power causing me to struggle in vain in life, die Now in The Name of Jesus

Let all my movements And Actions this year be directed by God in The Name of Jesus

Any Evil Broom sweeping away my blessings, catch fire, Burn to Ashes, in The Name of Jesus

PRAYER TO SURVIVE GLOBAL FAMINE AND ECONOMIC MELTDOWN

In times of trial, distress, famine and perplexity, faith is vital. True believers of old persevered until the end and never allowed threats of famine or lack of any degree to sweep off their faith. They believed and trusted God and were steadfast in the darkest hours, when all foundations on which men of the world built their hopes were collapsing.

> *"And the king called the Gibonites, and said unto them; (now the Gibonites were not of the children of Israel, but of the remnant of the Amorites; and the children of Israel had sworn unto them: and Saul sought to slay them in his zeal to the children of Israel and Judah"* (<u>2 Samuel 21:2</u>).

> *"[1]Now there cried a certain woman of the wives of the sons of the prophets unto Elisha, saying, Thy servant my husband is dead; and thou knowest that thy servant did fear the LORD: and the creditor is come to take unto him my two sons to be bondmen. [2]And Elisha said unto her, What shall I do for thee? tell me, what hast thou in the house? And she said, Thine handmaid hath not any thing in the house, save a pot of oil. [3]Then he said, Go, borrow thee vessels abroad of all thy neighbors, even empty vessels; borrow not a few. [4]And when thou art come in, thou shalt shut the door upon thee and upon thy sons, and shalt pour out into all those vessels, and thou shalt set aside that, which is full. [5]So she went from him, and shut the door upon her and upon her sons, who brought the vessels to her; and she poured out. [6]And it came to pass, when the vessels were full, that she said unto her son, Bring me yet a vessel. And he said unto her, There is not a vessel more. And the oil stayed. [7]Then she came and*

told the man of God. And he said, Go, sell the oil, and pay thy debt, and live thou and thy children of the rest" (2 Kings 4:1-7).

Most people, including believers, take wrong decisions in times of economic problems. Our faith is a precious and priceless treasure, which we must hold fast. Nothing is worth giving up your faith for. If you can wait for God and endure until the end, He will surely visit you and prosper you so that you never lack again.

"[43]*And the LORD gave unto Israel all the land which he sware to give unto their fathers; and they possessed it, and dwelt therein.* [44]*And the LORD gave them rest round about, according to all that he sware unto their fathers: and there stood not a man of all their enemies before them; the LORD delivered all their enemies into their hand.* [45]*There failed not ought of any good thing which the LORD had spoken unto the house of Israel; all came to pass"* (Joshua 21:43-45).

Between Egypt and the Promised Land, the children of Israel had many battles to fight. You must believe and trust God for provisions as you fight your battles until the end.

PRAYER POINTS

1. Any arrow of hardship fired into the world, I am not your candidate, in the name of Jesus.

2. I command any universal curse in my life to depart from me now, in the name of Jesus.

3. I set myself free from the consequences of the leader's mistakes, in the name of Jesus.

4. I break and loose myself from sins and mistakes of others, in the name of Jesus.

5. You, my personal mistake that has led me into poverty, be terminated, in the name of Jesus.

6. O Lord, arise and deliver me from generational curse of hardship, in the name of Jesus.

7. Every enemy of my joy, die by force, in the name of Jesus.

8. I walk out from global economic hardship, in the name of Jesus.

9. O Lord, arise and bless me in the midst of failures, in the name of Jesus.

10. Any spirit of suffering attacking my destiny, I cast you out, in the name of Jesus.

11. Any ancestral handwriting working against my life, be wiped all over, in the name of Jesus.

12. Any evil wind that is blowing all over the world, avoid me by force, in the name of Jesus.

13. Any covenant of poverty assigned to torment my life, break, in the name of Jesus.

14. Any evil hand upon this world, dry up in my life, in the name of Jesus.

15. Let the emptier of good things fail woefully in my life, in the name of Jesus.

16. Any power that has bewitched the world, release me by force, in the name of Jesus.

17. Any evil messenger from the devil into the world, I reject your message, in the name of Jesus.

18. Let evil powers eating up the peace of this world fail in my life, in the name of Jesus.

19. Any satanic decision to bring me into financial bondage, be frustrated, in the name of Jesus.

20. I arise and shine by the grace of God, in the name of Jesus.

21. Any wicked stronghold in the universe, I pull you down, in the name of Jesus.

22. Any power from the pit of hell that has entered into my garden, I chase you out, in the name of Jesus.

23. O Lord, renew my strength to fight until the end, in the name of Jesus.

24. No problem on earth will intimidate me, in the name of Jesus.

25. Any new problem that devil wants to introduce in this world, I overcome you, in the name of Jesus.

26. Let all my foes bow before my God forever, in the name of Jesus.

27. Any problem that is growing taller and fatter than me, I reduce you to nothing, in the name of Jesus.

28. Let devourers of my efforts in life die mysteriously, in the name of Jesus.

29. Any evil design to frustrate the world, be wasted, in the name of Jesus.

30. Any agent of demotion, demote yourself by force, in the name of Jesus.

31. Any demonic decision against my joy, fail woefully, in the name of Jesus.

32. I refuse to lose my ground to the devil, in the name of Jesus.

33. Any serpent in the garden of my life, die by force, in the name of Jesus.

34. O Lord, give me a miracle that will disgrace the economic meltdown, in the name of Jesus.

35. Any evil power mocking the people of God, be disgraced, in the name of Jesus.

36. Let all global impossibilities bow by force, in the name of Jesus.

37. O Lord, arise and deliver us from economic meltdown, in the name of Jesus.

38. I withdraw the authority of the devil over the world and my life, in the name of Jesus.

39. Let my breakthrough confound world leaders, in the name of Jesus.

40. Let my prosperity overflow the world boundaries, in the name of Jesus.

41. Every inherited poverty and debts, I demolish your motion, in the name of Jesus.

42. Any voice of economic problem in my life, be silenced forever, in the name of Jesus.

43. I command my mountains to convert to miracles, in the name of Jesus.

44. O Lord, use me to wipe the tears of the world, in the name of Jesus.

45. Let the secret and the strength of global economic meltdown be discovered and destroyed, in the name of Jesus.

46. My prosperity will not be a history while I am still alive, in the name of Jesus.

47. Lord Jesus, arise and connect me to the heaven's bank, in the name of Jesus.

48. Any power that has arrested the world's peace and prosperity, release it and die, in the name of Jesus.

49. I command all dead economies to resurrect, in the name of Jesus.

50. Let the hammer of the Almighty break the head of the world's serpent, in the name of Jesus.

51. I command the backbone of my problems to give up the ghost, in the name of Jesus.

52. Let the effect of my prayers kill every living problem on earth now, in the name of Jesus.

53. Blood of Jesus, empower me to revive the economy of this world, in the name of Jesus.

54. Anything the devil has brought into this world, catch fire and burn to ashes, in the name of Jesus.

55. Every satanic padlock against my deliverance, break now, in the name of Jesus.

Other titles in this series – ALONE WITH GOD

1. **Prayers for Good Health**

Prayers in this series include prayers to overcome asthma, diabetes, high blood pressure, surgeries, cancer, brain tumor, ectopic and prolong pregnancies, facial disease, fibroid and evil plantations, heart enlargement, incurable diseases, insanity, mental illness, sleeplessness, ulcers, heart disease, safe delivery, strokes, kidney problem, pneumonia, fever, poison, demonic burns, dog bite poisons, diarrhea, epilepsy, toothache and breast lump.

2. **Prayers for Financial Breakthrough**

Prayers in this series include prayers for financial assistance, finance breakthrough, financial miracles, divine breakthrough and opportunities, divine connections, business breakthrough, divine promotion, prosperity, protection from enemies, protection from evil, deliverance from poverty, overcoming enemies in the place of work, paying bills, prospering in business, divine connections, prospering in foreign land, recovering lost businesses, recovering a lost job, recovering all your loss, reviving collapsed or collapsing business, revoking evil decrees, rise from defeat, searching and finding jobs, stopping determined enemies, succeeding where others are failing and prayers to survive economic meltdown/famine.

3. **Prayers for Marriage & Family**

Prayers in this series deal with attacks at home, polygamous spirit, eating and having sex in dreams, having sex outside marriage, sexual weaknesses among legally married couples, broken homes, husbands who experience hatred from their wives, people who become sexually active with outsiders only, people who become sexually weak before their spouse, families in distress, men who are captured by strange women, true friendship, a godly woman, men who are sexually disconnected from their wives, women who experience hatred from their husbands, women who trust God for a child at old age, bear godly children, end a spirit marriage, become fertile and productive, deliver your children, frustrate divorce plans, keep your pregnancy, prevent miscarriage, end prolonged pregnancy, end separation plans, stop the enemies of your marriage and prayers to overcome troubles in your marriage.

4. **Prayers against Satanic Oppression**

Prayers in this series include prayers for protection from evil spirits, overcoming hopelessness, against all odds, arrows in the dream, attacks on churches, bewitchment, the spirit of confusion, marine curses, marine covenants, natural disasters, opposition at the work place, destroyers of environments, attacks in the dream, graveyard spirits, the power of sin, unknown enemies, overturn your defeats, disengage evil partners, overcome stress, crush witchcraft attacks, cross over to the next level, close witchcraft doors, cast out sexual demons, cast out demon of epilepsy and prayers to burn satanic liabilities.

5. **Prayers for Children & Youth**

Prayers in this series include prayers for bachelors and spinsters, before birthday, 3 days prayer for school children, children whose parents are divorced, victory at all cost, young school children, youths and teenagers, train children well.

6. **Prayers for Overcoming Attitude Problems**

Prayers in this series include prayers to overcome drug addiction, avoid criminal records, outlive death threats, overcome destructive habits, overcome fearful and intimidating problems, frustrations, deal with kidnappers and prayers to overcome evil habits.

7. **Prayers for Academic Success**

Prayers in this section include prayers for success in examination, prayers before examination, during examination, after examination, prayers for breakthrough in examination, prayers before an interview and prayer for undergraduates.

8. **Prayers for A Successful Career**

Prayers in this series include prayers to keep your job and destiny, for footballers, career people, for great and immediate changes, for guidance, new job, for sportsmen and women, best employment, to be self or gainfully employed, for a better job, enter into a new place, excel above your masters, excel in a job interview, force your enemies out of comfort, force your enemies to bow, move God into action, open closed doors, unburden your burdens and prayer to win in competitions.

9. **Prayers for Deliverance**

Prayers in this series include prayers for deliverance, against evil marks, evil traditions, for family tree, break the seal of bondage, break the yoke of death, destroy evil delays, destroy evil movements in the body, destroy serpents in the body, against your sinful pasts, for peace of mind, total freedom, stop the wicked, stop future enemies

10. **Special Prayers in His Presence**

Prayers in this series include prayers to win court, hospital and police cases, prayer at new year eves, for Africa, blessings, citizenship, cleansing, comfort, compassion, confidence, courage, Good Friday, Easter Sunday morning, Easter Saturday, encouragement, journey mercies, fellowship, ministry, to be touched for Christ, for residence permits, right decisions, safety, security, sponsorship, United Nations, Valentine's day, to be selected among the eleven, to preserve America and prayers to overcome all unknown problems.

11. **Alone With God (Complete version)** – This is the complete version of the ten-part series of ALONE WITH GOD. This book can be a highly resourceful prayer companion in your libraries and prayer ministries.

Thank You So Much!

Beloved, I hope you enjoyed this book as much as I believe God has touched your heart today. I cannot thank you enough for your continued support for this prayer ministry.

I appreciate you so much for taking out time to read this wonderful prayer book, and if you have an extra second, I would love to hear what you think about this book.

Please, do share your testimonies with me by sending an email to me at pastor@prayermadueke.com, or in Facebook at www.facebook.com/prayer.madueke. I personally invite you also to my website at www.prayermadueke.com to view many other books I have written on various issues of life, especially on marriage, family, sexual problems and money.

I will be delighted to partner with you in organized crusades, ceremonies, marriages and Marriage seminars, special events, church ministration and fellowship for the advancement of God's Kingdom here on earth.

Thank you again, and I wish you nothing less than success in life.

God bless you.

Prayer M. Madueke

OTHER BOOKS BY PRAYER M. MADUEKE

- *21/40 Nights Of Decrees And Your Enemies Will Surrender*
- *Tears in Prison*
- *Confront And Conquer*
- *35 Special Dangerous Decrees*
- *The Reality of Spirit Marriage*
- *Queen of Heaven*
- *Leviathan the Beast*
- *100 Days Prayer To Wake Up Your Lazarus*
- *Dangerous Decrees To Destroy Your Destroyers*
- *The spirit of Christmas*
- *More Kingdoms To Conquer*
- *Your Dream Directory*
- *The Sword Of New Testament Deliverance*
- *Alphabetic Battle For Unmerited Favors*
- *Alphabetic Character Deliverance*
- *Holiness*
- *The Witchcraft Of The Woman That Sits Upon Many Waters*
- *The Operations Of The Woman That Sits Upon Many Waters*
- *Powers To Pray Once And Receive Answers*
- *Prayer Riots To Overthrow Divorce*
- *Prayers To Get Married Happily*
- *Prayers To Keep Your Marriage Out of Troubles*
- *Prayers For Conception And Power To Retain*
- *Prayer Retreat – Prayers to Possess Your Year*
- *Prayers for Nation Building*
- *Organized student in a disorganized school*
- *Welcome to Campus*
- *Alone with God (10 series)*

CONTACTS

AFRICA

#1 Babatunde close,
Off Olaitan Street, Surulere
Lagos, Nigeria
+234 803 353 0599
pastor@prayermadueke.com,

#28B Ubiaja Crescent
Garki II Abuja,
FCT - Nigeria
+234 807 065 4159

IRELAND

Ps Emmanuel Oko
#84 Thornfield Square
Cloudalkin D22
Ireland
Tel: +353 872 820 909, +353 872 977 422
aghaoko2003@yahoo.com

EUROPE/SCHENGEN

Collins Kwame
#46 Felton Road
Barking
Essex IG11 7XZ GB
Tel: +44 208 507 8083, +44 787 703 2386, +44 780 703 6916
aghaoko2003@yahoo.com

Made in the USA
Lexington, KY
03 February 2015